THE
WORKING
WOMAN'S
GUIDE TO
REAL
SUCCESS

ELSA HOUTZ

D1710880

HARVEST HOUSE PU.
Eugene, Oregon 97402

THE WORKING WOMAN'S GUIDE TO REAL SUCCESS

Copyright © 1990 by Harvest House Publishers
Eugene, Oregon 97402

Library of Congress Cataloging-in-Publication Data

Houtz, Elsa. 1950-
    Working woman's guide to real success / Elsa Houtz.
    ISBN 0-89081-800-2
        1. Women—Religious life.   2. Success—Religious aspects—
    Christianity.   3. Women—Employment.   4. Women—Conduct
    of life.
    I. Title.
    BV4527.H69   1990
    248.8'43—dc20   89-26694
                                                                  CIP

Printed in the United States of America.

To the glory of God
and
to my sister, Jackie,
who is successful in so many ways

Contents

PART ONE

*About Traveling
First-Class*

CHAPTER 1

I Love a Happy Ending

They said to him,
"Please inquire of God
to learn whether our journey
will be successful."
The priest answered them,
"Go in peace. Your journey
has the Lord's approval."
—Judges 18:5,6

Katherine always flies first-class. She stows her expensive carry-on bag in the overhead luggage compartment along with her raincoat, and keeps her leather briefcase open on her lap so she can work during the flight. Seeing her makes you wonder if you've accidentally walked in on the shooting of an airline commercial showing how the airlines cater to executive women.

Katherine earns a six-figure salary, wears gorgeous clothes, and has two storybook children plus a supportive husband. Her job with a prestigious national firm involves traveling around the country consulting with top executives of major companies. She and her husband have just bought an old Victorian house that they're making plans to remodel into their dream home.

Did I mention that she also has an MBA from Harvard

and a PhD in psychology from Stanford, and is tall, thin, and beautiful besides?

* * *

Wow—what a success story! Wouldn't you say that Katherine is someone who has it all?

Let's look at the things that make Katherine seem such a perfect example of today's successful woman:

- Impressive salary
- Glamorous career involving travel and powerful contacts
- Husband and children
- Dream home
- Expensive wardrobe
- Attractive appearance
- High-level education
- Intelligence and competence

Quite an impressive list of qualifications for Successful Woman of the Year, isn't it?

Katherine is a real person, although that's not her real name. I sat next to her on a flight from Dallas to Los Angeles last spring. There had been a mix-up concerning my seat assignment on the overbooked flight, so the exasperated ticket agent gave up and assigned me a seat in first class. (I told him I could live with that.)

That's how I happened to be sitting in roomy, leather-upholstered luxury, telling the flight attendant I wanted my steak cooked medium-well, when Katherine boarded the plane.

Now there, I thought as I looked at her, *is a woman who belongs in first class.*

Katherine and I struck up a conversation during the flight, and I learned a great deal about her. She was a gracious and interesting woman, comfortable with her own accomplishments but not unduly impressed by them. In fact, when I suggested to Katherine that she must feel like she had attained a high degree of success in her life, she actually seemed surprised.

"I guess I don't think of it in terms of success," she said. "I love my work; it's very challenging and satisfying, even though there's a lot of pressure and it can be very stressful. But success . . . I don't know. Success for me is, well . . . for example, with this house we've bought. I think I'll feel a sense of success when we complete each stage in the remodeling process—like each time we finish a room, or when we get all the wallpapering done, or when some part of the house is finished and looks really great."

Wait a minute, I thought. Here's a woman who looks like she just stepped out of *Success Illustrated*, and when I ask her about success, she starts talking about wallpaper! Of all people, surely *she* ought to know what success is!

It's funny, though. Katherine and I talked about a lot of things during that long flight to Los Angeles, not just about her accomplishments. She talked about a failed marriage several years earlier, about feeling rejected and unloved and unlovable, about the sense of being a failure at the most important relationship in her life. She talked about being hurt by other people whom she trusted, and being let down by people she thought had her interests at heart. She told me of experiences in which she had been treated unfairly and cruelly by employers and co-workers. And she talked about being away from her children so much in order to meet the demands of her job.

"I travel three or four times a month," she said, "usually for three or four days each. I'm gone a lot."

"Who takes care of your children?" I asked.

"Well, we have a full-time person who lives with us, and my husband is a musician, so his hours are different from mine, and he can be there sometimes when I'm not . . . but I still feel guilty about not being there. I guess that's part of the price you pay for having a job like mine. I try to keep things in balance, but it still nags at me. Maybe it's not fair to my children . . . I don't know. Sometimes I just feel torn in half, or like I'm not doing the important things in my life very well. . . ."

If I had started the conversation by asking Katherine, "Do you consider yourself a successful woman?" I'm not at all sure she would have answered "yes." Perhaps her personal definition of success doesn't have anything to do with salary or position or clothes or accomplishments. Maybe to her it's something else.

How about you? What's your definition of success? What would it take for you to say "I'm a successful woman"?

Let's look at two more success stories.

Janice

Janice's watch works only occasionally. It's old, but she needs to wear one, and she can't afford a new one. She would like to have some new clothes, too—maybe just one really great outfit for work—but there's no room in the budget for that, either.

When her husband deserted her and her two children a year ago, she went to work for a temporary placement agency until she could sort out her options. Since she's an outgoing, people-oriented person, Janice likes working for lots of different companies and meeting all kinds of people. Her job as a "temp" suits her perfectly most of the time—except, maybe, at times like that stretch last winter.

It was flu season, and she was on a three-month clerical assignment with an insurance agency. Inevitably, she (like everyone around her) fell victim to the flu. Her throat felt like it had been sewn shut, her eyes burned, and her head felt packed with sawdust. Looking in the mirror, she saw a red-nosed, bleary-eyed woman who looked like she hadn't slept all night (which she hadn't).

Makeup didn't seem to help a bit, and her outdated, drab clothes certainly couldn't be counted on to give her appearance a lift.

That afternoon when she was at work, she looked and sounded so miserable that one of the supervisors said, "Janice, why don't you go home? You're just too sick to be at work."

"I can't afford to go home," she told him. "If I don't put in all my hours here, I don't get paid, and I can't afford not to receive a full paycheck. I'm sorry; I'll try not to make everyone else miserable, too!"

*   *   *

Hold it. There must be some mistake. Surely this isn't a success story. Let's look at the facts:

1. This woman is barely getting by financially.
2. She's rearing her children alone as a single parent.
3. Her job is temporary and not what you would call exciting.
4. Her clothes are all old and out of style.
5. She has the flu and can't even stay home to be sick.

If this person is an example of success, the dictionary must have it wrong.

Actually, there's more to Janice's story. For one thing, she did get over the flu. After considering her options, she decided to move back to Baltimore to be near her family as soon as the kids were out of school for the summer.

However, Janice's supervisor at the insurance agency was so impressed by Janice's work, her ability to get along with everyone, and her capable approach to handling the high-pressure office that he offered Janice a full-time job at an unheard-of salary. He practically begged Janice to change her plans and not move back to Baltimore.

One of Janice's co-workers grew so fond of her that she knitted Janice a sweater simply as a gesture of friendship.

Yet Janice went ahead with her plans to move. The office staff had a going-away party for her, which they had never before done for a temporary. Imagine Janice's surprise when she was presented with a gift from "the gang": a new watch!

After she had moved back to Baltimore, Janice and her children stayed with relatives while she looked for a job. "I've had some offers," she told a friend on the phone, "but none of them really would have enabled me to make the amount of money I need. Turning them down was tough, but I'm really trusting God to lead me into the right job situation—one that will meet my financial needs and be right in other ways too. I'm just so confident that He's in control. I know He has the right job in mind for me."

A few weeks later Janice reported to her friend that she was working as an executive secretary to the administrator of a large hospital. The man and his wife had "adopted" Janice and her children like part of their own family, and had helped her become settled in her new situation.

If you asked Janice what success meant to her, she would say, "It's achieving a goal and having the peace of knowing that that's God's will for you."

Money is still tight in Janice's household, and being a parent—especially a single parent—is never an easy task. Her wardrobe still isn't going to win any fashion awards. But in spite of those things, I think Janice would say her story is a success story after all.

Sarah

Sarah never planned to have children. She and her husband, a teacher, lead busy and active lives centered around their jobs, their common interest in traveling, and their involvement in church and community activities. Sarah's public-relations work challenges and excites her. She loves the diversity and the creativity, and being around other dynamic, fast-moving people keeps her own energy level high.

When she found out she was pregnant, she really wanted to be happy, but she had some major adjustments to make first. She had always thought life would go on indefinitely just the way it was. She took her independence for granted. If a business trip came up at the last second, she was off! If a meeting lasted late into the night, no problem. If she and her husband heard about a great new weekend getaway spot, Friday afternoon would find them on the road.

But now—a baby! Diapers, responsibilities, schedules, school, braces, chicken pox!

"I guess life wasn't meant to be predictable," she tells herself, but she still wonders how she'll cope with this enormous change in her life.

Most people in the business world talk about success in terms of "climbing the ladder." You work your way up, rung by rung, paying your dues, watching for opportunities to move up, playing by the rules of the corporate game. When Sarah found out she was pregnant, she felt like she had just fallen off the ladder completely.

The baby came, and she tried hard not to feel resentful that her career had been short-circuited. The people with whom she had worked told her it was a shame that such a promising career was jeopardized by this unexpected development. After all, how could she handle the intense demands of her job if she was preoccupied worrying about a baby at home?

Sarah loved the baby, whom she named Jeremy, deeply. She was glad that life had held that particular surprise for her, although there were many days when she missed the stimulation of her work and the sense of worth it gave her. She found that she longed to talk to other adults and get a break from the routines of motherhood. She felt guilty when she had those feelings, and wondered if she was a bad mother because of them.

When the baby was several months old, Sarah began receiving calls from people she knew in the business community who wondered when she was going back to work. Although it was hard to do, she told them she really felt that she needed to stay home with her baby, at least for a couple of years. She was pleasantly surprised when they responded by asking her if she would work for them freelance, out of her home, just handling a few specific projects now and then.

It turned out to be the best of both worlds. Sarah sets her own hours, working around the baby's schedule, and sometimes asks a friend or relative to babysit if there's an important meeting or a short deadline on a project. She feels that she's giving her best to her child, and at the same time she's continuing to do the work she enjoys.

Maybe it's not the arrangement she'll want forever, but for now it's perfect. No, she may not be rocketing up the career ladder, but is she successful?

"At this time in my life, under these circumstances, in light of the priorities I've set—yes!"

Obviously, success is something different for Katherine, for Janice, and for Sarah. And I believe that it's something different for you and me, too. As we think about success and what we need to do to attain it, we have several choices.

1. We can accept the traditional definitions of success that the world sets before us—money, power, position, possessions, glitter, and glamour—and spend our lives striving for more and more of those things, constantly comparing ourselves to other people to see who's ahead in the race.

2. We can decide that we don't have the talent, the skills, the education, the background, or the ability to be

"successful," and that success is therefore something meant for other people rather than for us.

3. We can adopt a whole separate standard of success—a biblical standard—and in so doing, begin a lifelong process of discovering the real success that God wants for us. When we do that, we accept the promise of freedom in Christ, freedom from the necessity of doing and being all the things the world tells us are necessary to make us successful.

Each of us, as we seek to live the life God intends for us, has the chance to pursue a special and unique kind of success, tailor-made for us by the One who knows us best, the One who created us and has given us a vitally important role to fulfill in this world. The success He has designed for us is just waiting to become a part of our lives, but before we can grasp it, we have to make some fundamental decisions about ourselves and our relationship to Him and to the world around us. We need to understand some things about who we are and why we are here, and what God has called us to do.

Katherine talked about success being a *process* rather than a *goal*. In the same vein, I like to think of it as a *journey* rather than a *destination*. I believe that in God's kingdom as we know it here on earth, success lies along the way, and we experience it as we live for Him in this world and as He reveals more and more of Himself to us.

When I consider that journey, it gives me a sense of excitement—a joyful confidence that wherever the journey takes me, I will travel with meaning and purpose rather than wandering aimlessly through a maze of false standards and uncertain goals.

The journey will be different for each of us, and I think there's a good chance that we won't even know when we get there. Success will come to us in ways that we, with our limited vision, cannot even imagine right now.

To start the journey, let's look at what success is—and isn't.

POINTS OF INTEREST

Points of Interest are notes at the end of each chapter that record your ideas, reactions, feelings, experiences, and goals. As you work through this book, proceeding through the journey that we talked about, the Points of Interest will help you chart your course. Then, when the trip is over, you'll have a written record of where you've been in terms of your thinking about success.

1. Off the top of your head, name the most successful person you know (don't think about it for a long time—just respond!).

Bryan

Now list three or four criteria that explain why you consider that person successful.

He likes his job   _He EARNS A good SALARY_

He does it well   _He is well Respected_

2. Right now, what does success mean to you? Write a general definition.

Enjoying what I do, having money to do what's important to me, doing something worthwhile

3. List one or more things that, if you attained them, would make you feel more successful than you feel now:

_____

_____

4. If the Bible contained a point-blank definition of success, what do you think it would be?

_____

SIGNPOST

Signposts are specially selected Scripture verses that bear on our task of understanding the nature of real success. You'll find them at various points in each chapter. If you memorize each one as it occurs in the book, they will become your own landmarks to guide you on your way. At those times when the journey seems confusing and the choices aren't clear, these spiritual "arrows" will be a welcome source of inspiration and direction.

> *O Lord, you have searched me*
> *and you know me. You know when I sit*
> *and when I rise; you perceive*
> *my thoughts from afar.*
> *You discern my going out*
> *and my lying down;*
> *you are familiar with all my ways.*
>
> —Psalm 139:1-3

CHAPTER 2

Basketball, Office Furniture, and the New York Marathon

S-U-C-C-E-S-S!
That's the way you spell success!
Who will have it? Can you guess?
Our team, our team, yes, yes, YES!
—High school basketball cheer,
circa 1963

At high school basketball games, it was pretty easy to figure out what the cheerleaders meant by "success" when they cheered on the team. Whoever won the game succeeded, and whoever lost the game didn't. Every year in my hometown, on the morning after the final game of the state basketball tournament, the newspapers would run a photo of the losing team's tearful cheerleaders, exhausted and despondent, disappointed by the unsuccessful pursuit of that particular brand of success.

That's one of the problems with the idea of success as "winning"—that is, as doing better at something than someone else. If you invest a lot of time and energy pursuing this, and then, when all is said and done, you still don't have it, then you've "lost." You're a loser. You've been defeated, beaten. You're not as good as the other guy.

Spending our lives comparing ourselves with others is an exercise in frustration and sorrow. No matter how hard we try or how good we are at something, there is always someone smarter, richer, more athletic, more talented, or more beautiful than we are. When we are always competing, always trying to win by doing better than someone else, we spend our lives striving, never relaxing, never rejoicing in someone else's achievement, never savoring our own accomplishments just for themselves.

Yet it's tempting. I know, because four years ago I joined an extremely strenuous self-defense class that involved hours and hours of practice and fitness training. Never having been an athlete by any stretch of the imagination, I found the exhausting workouts and numerous techniques a real challenge. Even after a couple of years, everything was still very difficult for me. I looked around at the other men and women in the class and saw how easily some of them learned new techniques, and how smoothly they performed them, and I became discouraged.

"I look at those other people," I whined to my friend Barbara, "and I know I'll never be as good as they are. It's so discouraging. No matter how hard I work or how much I train, I'll never have the technique or the form they have. Their natural ability is just so much greater than mine."

"Have you learned a lot since you first started taking the class?" she asked.

"Of course! I've trained six hours a week for two years! I've learned an incredible amount."

"Then why don't you focus on how far you've come from where you started," she said, "instead of on how much better someone else is than you?"

I felt foolish because Barbara was so right. My idea of "succeeding" in that class had been to be better than everyone else—even though, realistically, that wasn't even a remote possibility! My competitive attitude had led to frustration and discouragement in what was basically a satisfying and enjoyable activity.

Believe it or not, I'm still in that class. I'm still no athlete, and there are a lot of other people who do things much better than I do, but I'm proud of what I've learned and what I've accomplished. I enjoy watching the beautiful form and technique of other people in the class, and I try to constantly learn from them. I've learned that I don't have to be better than others to be "successful." I just want to be better than I was yesterday.

SIGNPOST

Each one
should test his own actions.
Then he can take pride in himself,
without comparing himself to somebody else,
for each one should carry his own load.

—Galatians 6:4,5

I learned firsthand that equating success with winning—which places us in constant competition with others—is a risky proposition. But what about other popular definitions of success?

Is Success a Big Office?

A few years ago I had a business appointment at the office of a man who is in the advertising business. Never having visited his firm's suite of offices before, I was dazzled when I entered their reception area: ornate chandeliers ... flamboyant silk flower arrangements ... enormous chrome-and-glass tables ... huge, upholstered armchairs.

"Your offices are certainly, uh, attractive," I told him.

"Well," he said, "we could do the work just as well in an airplane hangar, but this impresses the clients."

Being in the image-building business, he and his associates were well aware that the impression of success is extremely important in the commercial world. People want to do business with a firm that appears to be successful, and expensive-looking decor is one way for a firm to say "We're successful" to its potential clients.

The same line of thinking often applies to our perception of individuals as successful or unsuccessful. If a man or woman has the right "decor," then we figure he or she must be successful. We equate success with the *trappings* of success.

What "decor" tells us that a woman is successful?

- A classy-sounding job?
- A wardrobe in which everything goes together?
- 2.5 bright, beautiful children?
- A tall, blond husband with a tan?
- A house straight out of a decorating magazine?
- A fat paycheck and a thin figure?
- A car in the price range of "If you have to ask how much it is, you can't afford it"?
- All of the above?

These are all things that, in our society, create the impression of success. Remember Katherine, in Chapter 1? She certainly had all the right "decor."

Just as equating success with winning has its drawbacks, so equating success with certain material or personal acquisitions also has its pitfalls, as summed up by the story of Job in the Bible. Job had it all, but then Job lost it all. One of the few certainties of life is that wealth, material possessions, physical beauty, and even relationships simply do not last. To rely on those things to define ourselves or others as successful is a shaky foundation indeed.

SIGNPOST

Cast but a glance at riches, and they are gone,
for they will surely sprout wings
and fly off to the sky like an eagle.
—Proverbs 23:5

Is Success Having People Say "How High?" When You Say "Jump!"?

The first time I ever taught a journalism class at the local college, I was terrified. It wasn't that I didn't know the material or didn't feel qualified to teach it; it was that here were these 20 students, dependent on me not only for their grades but also for the knowledge and skills they were supposed to obtain in my class. If I gave them failing grades, or I didn't teach them what they needed to know to continue in that field, it could affect the whole course of their lives. The idea of having that kind of power over them scared me silly.

It's common in today's world, however, to view power over other people as a measure of success: having control over people's jobs or the course of their careers; being in a position to influence the actions of a community or a government; making decisions that affect huge numbers of people. The theory goes that the more people's lives you affect, or the more resources you control, or the more money you manage, the more successful you are. Or perhaps it's that the more far-reaching the effect of your actions, the more successful you are.

Like the previous definitions of success that we've discussed, defining success as power is risky, and I think it's risky because it makes the *extent* of a person's influence more important than the *quality* of his or her influence.

For example, a woman who rises to a senior management position with a major national company would certainly be considered successful because of the extent of her influence. But what about the *quality* of that influence? What does she do to insure that the people who work for that company are treated with fairness and respect? What programs does she initiate to improve life in the community, or to protect our environment, or to address any of the myriad problems of our world through the resources of her position?

Surely a person in such an influential position could do a great deal of good. Yet if power is our only criterion for success, then that person will be viewed as successful whether her influence results in good or evil. Is that the kind of success we want to emulate—success that leads to influence but sets no standards for the quality of that influence?

And what about the person who has a crucial and positive influence on just one other life? Is that person not a success? Think of the high school teacher who encouraged you to pursue your dreams or who saw potential in you that even you didn't see; the minister or Christian friend who set you on the path to new life; the parents who made sacrifices so that you would have opportunities they never had. The *quality* of their influence, not its extent, was great. Are these people less successful than the person whose influence affects thousands of others but makes no lasting difference in those lives?

Is Success Crossing the Finish Line?

We've talked about success in terms of winning, of material gain, and of power. But what about success as reaching a goal?

Jan grew up in New York City. She moved to another state over 15 years ago, but she was still a New Yorker at heart. (If nothing else, her accent always gave her away.) She was also a runner, and her dream was to run the New York City Marathon. She knew she didn't have a chance of placing, but she wanted to finish the race. She wanted to cross that line.

Finally, at age 36, she decided to do it. She trained for nearly a year, building up her endurance and increasing her distance week by week.

The weekend of the race came, and she traveled to New York City and ran in the Marathon. And she finished. She even has a photo of herself crossing the finish line, arms raised in victory. Success!

Later, when a friend congratulated her on her accomplishment and asked her how it felt, she said, "After it was all over, this little voice just kept saying, 'Well, I've done it. So what?' "

Jan's dream had come true, but it didn't give her the sense of satisfaction she had expected. She had been successful at meeting her goal, but she didn't feel like a successful person. What was the problem?

1. Goal-based success is a moving target.

Think of a time in your life when you really wanted to achieve something specific, something that, if you achieved it, would make you feel like a success. Maybe it was making the basketball team or the school orchestra. Or maybe it was landing that first job in your chosen field, or just a better job than the one you had. Or buying your first house, or having a magazine publish a poem you had written. Maybe it was getting married or having a child.

Do you remember feeling that if you could just attain that one goal, cross that one finish line, you'd be on top of the world? But what happened after you met that goal? The orchestra's final concert ended. You became discontented in your job and started looking for one that paid more and had more responsibility. Your "dream house" was suddenly too small or too shabby. Having just one poem published didn't seem like much when you considered that some people had whole books of them published. Perhaps a marriage lost its spark or a child grew up.

Human beings are not by nature contented. How many people do you know who could say, "I like my life the way it is; I'm happy with things just as they are"? Could you honestly say this?

We always look for greener pastures, more noteworthy accomplishments, more money, better jobs, nicer neighborhoods, a more rewarding relationship . . . sometimes even a spouse that we think will meet our needs better than the one we have. The dream that seemed so all-important long ago is just a dim memory, and we wonder how it could have been so consuming at the time.

There's certainly nothing wrong with wanting to make our lives better—for ourselves, our children, our communities, our country, the world. Setting our sights higher and higher gives us a sense of challenge and the possibility of accomplishment. A healthy discontent with the status quo is what spurs people to new levels of achievement; it produces more advanced technology, better ways of fighting disease, more beautiful works of art, and faster, safer transportation. In fact, in the next chapter we'll be looking at how we can use our goals to help us attain our dreams to chart our journey toward success.

The danger lies in defining ourselves as successful or unsuccessful *only* on the basis of crossing those moving "finish lines." When we do that, we set ourselves up for a lifelong roller-coaster ride, filled with "highs" of short-lived happiness and long stretches of chronic discontent.

2. Goal-based success leaves us asking, "What happens next?"

When you reach the goal you set, after the struggle is over and the challenge has been met, then what? Interviews with men and women who have reached the top of the business world have shown that often, after reaching the top, they're left—like Jan—with a sense of emptiness, a lack of purpose, a voice inside asking, "What do I do now?" The pursuit of their goals was the focus of their lives, and once the goals were all behind them, there was nothing to look forward to. What a sad way to live the remaining years of your life, feeling that it held no more challenges for you, no more excitement!

I once knew a man who had been a fighter pilot in World War II. By the age of 20 he had become one of the nation's most skilled and most decorated aviators. Then the war ended, and he went home. He bought a small business and raised a family. But there was always an underlying sense of discontent, a feeling that life was all downhill. As an aviator, measuring success by his skill in combat, he was a winner. He was one of the very best. He crossed the finish line again and again. Afterward, though, as a man living an ordinary, day-to-day life of mortgage payments and car problems and children with the flu, he never saw himself as a success again.

3. Goal-based success tells us, "If you don't succeed, you've failed."

In this definition of success, either you cross the finish line or you don't. There are no degrees of success, no points for second best. Anything that isn't success is failure. So we struggle and strive and devote all our energies to crossing that line, fearing the failure that we'll have to deal with if we don't make it. In the process, our lives can become sorely out of balance. We become driven to achieve that one current goal, and we miss out on the joys of other important aspects of our lives.

These goals aren't confined to the business world, either. I know women who are so committed to being "successful" mothers that they strive and strain just as much toward that goal as any woman who has career ambitions outside the home. They pour everything they have into their children, and if a child disappoints them or fails to live up to their standards, then they feel overwhelmed by failure. They haven't met their goal, so they feel they must have failed.

I wonder if those of us who are mothers sometimes foster these definitions of success—success as winning, as material gain, as power, as reaching goals—in our children. We pressure them to earn good grades, do well at sports or other school activities, attend a good college, and land a good job. In doing so we may be paving the way for our children to experience all the pitfalls we've just talked about, as they go through life in pursuit of "success." Perhaps as we work to arrive at our own new definition of success, we can pass along to them what we've learned.

Recently I read an article about the increasing number of women starting and running their own businesses. The article quoted a woman who had just opened a small specialty restaurant. After holding a variety of other jobs and experiencing a series of ups and downs in her personal life, she had decided to start her own business. She expressed optimism and excitement about her new venture, but she maintained a healthy perspective on its success: "If I failed," she said, "I'd never call it a failure anyway. I'd call it a learning experience!" What a refreshing viewpoint! I wonder how many of the nation's estimated 5 million women who own businesses would echo her philosophy? What do you think?

Is Success "Making It" in a Man's World?

The equal-rights movement, now over two decades old, has had a major influence on women's thinking about success. In the effort to attain equality in the workplace, women have found it necessary to accept the same standards and rules that have governed men in the workplace. This includes adopting the measures of success that have traditionally been applied to men— position, influence, power, wealth—as well as taking on other measures such as physical appearance, parental accomplishments, and the ability to juggle home and career demands. Only now are women beginning to ask: Is this what I really want? Does this represent success for *me*? Is this God's desire?

Women are finding, like Katherine did, that success as defined by the business world exacts a heavy price. As we strive to prove ourselves in our jobs, we feel that we are failing as mothers. Guilt is our constant companion. We may shine on the job, but then we don't have the time or energy to do all the other things we'd like to do: cultivate and maintain friendships; create special, memorable experiences for our children; build a marriage relationship that will last a lifetime; discover new interests and talents within ourselves; develop a deep and lasting spiritual reservoir that will enable us to ride out life's changes with serenity and faith.

There is no doubt that women have what it takes to succeed in the workplace. But the questions that each of us needs to ask are: Is this right for me in terms of what God has created me to be and to do? Am I willing to pay the price, and am I willing to commit those I love to paying the price?

Is Success Being What Someone Else Is?

Jenny is a stay-at-home mother with two small children. She worked for several years as an executive secretary, but when her first child was born she felt she needed to stay at home, at least for a few years. She still believes she made the right choice, but she doesn't feel very successful. In the grocery store she'll see women on their way home from work whose shoes match their outfits and whose hair and makeup still look neat. She feels frumpy in her jeans and sneakers, and wishes she had done more with her hair than just pull it back in a barrette.

Well, you can tell they haven't been washing diapers and wiping runny noses all day! I'll bet they actually accomplished something important today—and now they can go home and relax. I just get to go home and wash more diapers and wipe more runny noses.

Jenny's self-image is at rock bottom. If you asked her if she is successful, she would probably laugh.

LeAnn is the assistant manager of a clothing store. She is a single parent with a seven-year-old daughter, so her job is essential. Since she gets a discount on clothes at the store, she's always wearing the most current styles and newest accessories, but making ends meet is a constant battle. Sometimes after work, before she picks up her daughter at the day-care center, she'll run into the grocery for a frozen pizza or some hamburger buns; she's too tired to cook anything more elaborate. Every now and then she sees a woman in there who she just knows doesn't have to work outside the home. The woman will be talking with her children, letting the kids help pick out groceries, helping them read the labels on the boxes. It's as though being at the store together is a family outing, not just another chore to squeeze into a hectic schedule.

I'll bet she doesn't have to dress up every day and deal with the public, LeAnn says to herself. *I spend more time with my customers than with my own daughter. I'd sure love to be able to be home when she comes home from school, and do special little things with her during the day. I'm always so tired after work I can't get up much enthusiasm for the games she wants to play or TV shows she wants to watch. I'm sure not going to win any Mother-of-the-Year contests!*

Jenny and LeAnn both feel like failures. Why? Because they're measuring success by someone else's life, comparing themselves unfavorably to someone whose life is different from theirs. It's as though Jenny is defining success in terms of LeAnn's life, and vice versa. It's the grass-is-always-greener syndrome: Jenny thinks she would feel more successful if she went to an outside job every day and "accomplished something." LeAnn thinks she would feel like a more successful mother if she didn't have to work outside the home.

When we define success in terms of the external circumstances of our lives, we're likely to spend most of our time feeling that we're lacking. Few people's lives are exactly the way they would like them to be. There are some things about our lives and ourselves that we can change and some things that we can't. If we define success only in terms of those circumstances that we *can't* change—that is, if we tell ourselves, "I'd be successful if only . . . ," knowing that the "if only" will never happen—then by doing so we rule out success as a possibility in our lives. Our journey toward success has ended before it has even begun.

I don't believe that God wants us to do this. First of all, God can change things that we cannot. He calls us to faith and hope, not to resignation and despair. All things are possible for Him.

Secondly, when we confine our definition of success to a certain set of worldly circumstances (such as working outside the home or being a stay-at-home mother or reaching a senior management position), we completely disregard the fact that God's standard for success has far more to do with what is *inside* us than what is *outside* us. His work in our lives and His plan for our success are not limited by the barriers and obstacles of circumstance—unless we allow that limitation to happen.

Is Success Being the Best at Being Yourself?

Several years ago, as part of an intensive, weeklong management training course, I took a battery of personality tests. After the tests had been scored, a psychologist reviewed them with me to help interpret what they told me about myself.

One of the most interesting things I learned from the test results is that I am a person who becomes bored easily (you know, like a 12-year-old whose summer vacation began a week ago); that is, I don't feel comfortable doing the same thing for very long.

That didn't surprise me. During the last 15 years I have worked for eight different employers—and that's not counting the three years I was in graduate school! Every time I was asked for my resumé, I felt embarrassed about the number of jobs I've had. My idea of a successful-looking resumé was one that showed a person had stayed with one company or in one field for a long time and had risen through the ranks in that company or that field. I thought prospective employers would look at my resumé and view me as unreliable, unstable, and unable to stick with anything I've started.

The psychologist who reviewed the tests with me pointed out that my frequent job changes are simply the reflection of a certain personality type. It's not better or worse than that of the person who stays in one job for a long time; it's just different. He encouraged me to continue exploring new job areas rather than try to "settle down," which was what I thought I needed to do to be "successful."

I felt liberated by that new knowledge of myself. My old definition of success as a steady climb up the corporate ladder might work for others, but not for me. I felt freed to pursue my many interests and seize new opportunities as they arose.

I believe popular psychology has helped many other people, as it did me, to look less outside themselves and more inside for their definitions of success. For many of these people, success is doing what makes you happy or being content with who and what you are, regardless of how that measures up to someone else's standards.

Needless to say, I'm very much in favor of this approach—but only up to a point. There is a pitfall even in this seemingly liberating definition of success. Just as it's hazardous to look at other people's lives or circumstances to define success (as Jenny and LeAnn did), it's also risky to look only within ourselves at our own needs.

When we define success in this way, we risk becoming fully self-centered, totally focused on our own wants and needs, concerned only with what feels best to us at the time, with what satisfies us and what makes us feel good about ourselves.

We live in a broken, angry, sad, hurting, hungry world. Every day, as we go about our business, we encounter people in need of our kindness, our love, our compassion, our generosity, our skills, and our talents. If we lose sight of them and their needs, and of the larger world and its needs, then we have lost sight of the responsibilities of dual citizenship: citizenship in the human race and citizenship in God's kingdom.

This inward-looking definition of success has a further danger, too: that we forget who it is that makes our achievements, and in fact our very existence, possible. We have life, families, relationships, possessions, the ability to work, and the skill to accomplish things *only because God graciously and lovingly allows us to have those things.* Part of our humanness is our constant forgetfulness, the ease with which we forget that God is the source of all that we are and have. Defining success solely by what satisfies our own needs tends to foster that forgetfulness.

In spite of God's continual warnings, the Israelite people repeatedly experienced the painful consequences of looking only within themselves for answers, of basing their decisions on what seemed best to them in their limited human understanding. One of the bleakest periods in Israel's history is chronicled in the Old Testament book of Judges, which sums up that period like this: "In those days Israel had no king; everyone did as he saw fit" (Judges 21:25).

If we define success only in terms of what we "see fit," then we lose out on the riches of God's wisdom and His guidance in finding our unique role in the world. We confine ourselves to a narrow life, limited by what we can see and do and understand. Only when we make God a partner in our quest for a personal, individualized meaning of success can we hope to attain a meaning that will bring us lasting peace and satisfaction.

This I'll-decide-what's-good-for-me approach to success has another pitfall, too: It throws off the balance between the needs of the individual and the needs of the body of Christ. Our respect for individual worth and dignity should not be used as an excuse for disregarding the rules that God has laid down for the entire community of believers.

Americans are traditionally a group of confirmed individualists. In what other country in the world can you glibly set fire to the flag, stand on a street corner and preach that an alien spaceship is coming to rescue the world, or publish a book enumerating the personal foibles of the nation's President and his family? We cherish the rights of the individual to speak freely, to think freely, to worship freely, to be governed by those we have chosen freely. Our legal system defends these rights regardless of whether any particular individual or group approves of the way they're expressed. We're willing to take a stand in the world community to see that these rights are protected, not just for us but for the people of other nations as well.

We fight in the courts to protect the access of every citizen to equal opportunities in education, in the workplace, in government. We believe in personal initiative, creativity, and individualism; we applaud the person who breaks the rules or thwarts the system in order to achieve a worthwhile end or find a better way of doing things—to succeed. We are a nation of revolutionaries.

I don't think the Christian fathers who founded this country anticipated that we would use this devoutly independent spirit as an excuse for ignoring our responsibilities as members of the body of Christ. The individual is not more important than the body; the body is more important than any individual, and the commandments that God has given us as a body of believers are not to be revised as we see fit to accommodate us. In contrast, our lives are to be revised to accommodate God's commandments.

I was in college in the late 1960's, when "Do your own thing" was the prevailing sentiment. The more weird a person could make her clothing, her speech, and even her behavior, the more "with it" she was. It was definitely a period in history when individualism was at its peak.

Even two decades later, I vividly remember the words of a visiting evangelist who preached to our collegiate fellowship group. "We live in an era of tolerance," he said, "but the fact is that Jesus was not tolerant. Jesus doesn't call us to do our own thing. He calls us to do *God's* thing."

God works in each of our lives differently. He has created each of us uniquely, to serve Him in a way no one else can. But the commandments He has laid down for us are the same for every Christian, not subject to change according to what we want or need. Yes, we are to live as revolutionaries—but not for our own ends or to make the world more to our own liking. Our revolution is to occur daily, weekly, and hourly as we seek change in our own lives and change to help bring about God's will in the world. If we are to succeed as individuals we must of necessity also succeed as members of the body of Christ.

POINTS OF INTEREST

1. What was the earliest definition of success that you were aware of as a child or a teenager?

_____

_____

2. How do you think each of the following people would define success for you (for *you*, not for themselves)?

Your mother: _____

Your boss: _____

Your spouse, if any: _____

Your children, if any: _____

Your best friend: _____

Someone with whom you work: _____

3. Which of the definitions above is closest to your own current definition of success for yourself? Why do you think that person's is closer than the others?

_____

_____

_____

4. In this chapter, we talked about success as measured by a variety of earthly standards. What are the pitfalls of each of these as the sole standard of success?

Success as winning: _____

Success as material gain: _____

Success as power: _____

Success as reaching goals: _____

Success as measuring up to male standards: _____

_____

Success as self-fulfillment/individuality: _____

_____

5. Among the people you know, including yourself, can you think of specific individuals who define success in one or more of these ways? Specifically, what do you think are their definitions of success, and how can you tell? How do you feel about their definitions? Would they work for you?

6. How do you think God measures success?

_____

_____

_____

SIGNPOST

He has showed you, O man, what is good.
And what does the LORD require of you?
To act justly and to love mercy and to
walk humbly with your God.
—Micah 6:8

Be careful that you do not forget the LORD
your God.
—Deuteronomy 8:11

CHAPTER 3

Welcome Aboard!

God does not ask your ability or inability;
He asks only your availability.

—Mary Kay Ash

In the last chapter we talked about definitions of success that don't work. To help us find one that does work, let's look at some examples of success in the Bible. We'll see what it has to teach us about the meaning of the word "success" and about successful people.

Who comes to mind when you consider successful women and men of the Bible? Certainly Jesus was "successful" as He carried out the work of salvation and changed the course of history forever. The apostle Paul was a successful evangelist, bringing Christ's message to far-flung parts of the world. And what about David, a successful military leader and a wise, powerful king whose people loved and revered him, or how about the young, beautiful Queen Esther, who successfully thwarted a plan to destroy the Jews?

There are many other men and women in the Bible to whom we can look for models of success: Moses, Ruth,

Joshua, Mary, Lydia, Timothy, and dozens more. One of the most successful people described in the Bible, though, doesn't even have a name. She is the "wife of noble character" described in Proverbs 31. (If you haven't met her, take a moment now to read Proverbs 31:10-31. You'll enjoy making her acquaintance!)

What can we learn from these great women and men of God that will help us chart our own journeys toward success? Volumes have been written about each of them. Where do we start? I think it's helpful to examine *their* journeys toward success from three aspects:

1. The task or tasks they were called to carry out; that is, their *work.*
2. The *goal(s)* they were trying to reach.
3. The *results* they desired.

Our day-to-day *work* shapes the specific route that our journey takes. *Goals* comprise the milestones along the way, the landmarks that tell us we're on the right track and are making progress. The *results* we hope our journeys will achieve represent the destination; they determine where we're headed.

When the word "success" appears in the Bible, its context suggests these three components: work, goals, and results. For example, Nehemiah felt a burning desire to rebuild the wall of Jerusalem, which had been destroyed by Isreal's enemies. The *work* itself was staggering: collecting and transporting the needed materials, fighting off the attacks of hostile tribes, recruiting the necessary manpower, and then actually building the new wall. His *goal* was to complete the rebuilding of the wall. The *result* he desired was to begin reestablishing Jerusalem as the holy city of his people—and he succeeded.

It's interesting to note that the word "success" does not appear in the New Testament, either in the King James Version or in the more modern translations. When

Jesus talked about the concept that we know as success, He talked about it only in terms of "greatness." He said that if we are to be great, we must learn to serve. So if we are to understand success from a biblical perspective, we must incorporate this vitally important concept of servanthood.

Both the Old Testament and the New Testament characters who succeeded in God's sight demonstrated servanthood. Their work, their goals, and the results they sought all reflected a desire to serve God and to serve other people. If there is one fundamental principle that the Bible identifies as essential to success, it is the principle of serving. (Later we'll look at how servanthood can be translated into daily living as we travel toward success.)

To better understand the Bible's definition of success, let's see how this three-part model—work, goals and results—was reflected in individual lives. The chart on the following page, Diagram 1, lists some aspects of each component as demonstrated in the lives of Mary, Jesus, Esther, Paul, and the Proverbs 31 woman. Analyzing their "success" in terms of these components illustrates some important principles for us to keep in mind as we proceed.

1. Our day-to-day work, the sum of the tasks we carry out, is an important part of our journey to success.

Often, we believe that only those activities we can label "spiritual" or "religious" are important to God. The Bible suggests otherwise.

For example, the apostle Paul worked with his hands (at tentmaking and other "nonreligious" jobs) to earn his keep when visiting the various churches he had founded. One of Queen Esther's primary tasks was to keep herself beautiful and desirable for the king. In the absence of electric curling irons, blow-dryers, and

Diagram 1

	Work (Route)	Goals (Milestones)	Desired Results (Destination)
Mary	Caring for children Maintaining home	See that her son received religious training Create an environment where Jesus could grow in "wisdom and in stature"	Live in a way worthy of the unique role that God called her to perform
Jesus	Preaching Teaching Healing	Train disciples Cause many to be saved Confront the religious leaders	Complete God's work of salvation
Esther (see Esther 5:1–8:17)	Preparing banquet for Haman and the king Presenting requests to the king	Destroy Haman Revoke Haman's decree	Save God's people from destruction
Apostle Paul	Preaching Training evangelists Working to earn his keep	Found new churches	Bring the gospel to places where it was unknown
Proverbs 31 woman (see Prov. 31:10–31)	Weaving fabrics Preparing food Purchasing household goods Buying and selling property	Bring credit to husband and children Have household prepared against future needs Help the needy	Be a woman of God, obeying His commandments

smudgeproof mascara, we can assume that this was a more time-consuming job than it is today (and it's time-consuming enough today!). Does that seem like a religious activity? Her plan to save the Jews could not have been carried out if she had not been in favor with the king, and her beauty was important to her success. The Proverbs 31 woman also had all kinds of "mundane" tasks to do—weaving, buying and selling, grocery shopping, supervising the household servants. (Later we'll look further at the role of work in our lives, and how our earthly work is related to God's work.)

2. *Our goals are the link between the things we do (our work) and the results we desire.*

As we discussed in the last chapter, setting goals and then viewing them as ends in themselves is self-defeating. Goals are merely a *means to an end.* They help us shape our day-to-day and year-to-year living in a way that will bring about the results we desire.

Our goals must be in harmony with our ultimate destination. For example, it's a contradiction for me to say, "My ultimate desire is to use my talents to the glory of God," and then to set a goal of making a million dollars so that I can have every material possession I want. Do I direct my day-to-day efforts toward the goal, or toward the ultimate result? Only if I bring the two into harmony can I set a course that will bring both of them about; otherwise, my journey will weave back and forth between various destinations, and I'm unlikely to ever arrive anyplace I want to be.

3. *We cannot attain success apart from the awareness of God in our lives.*

Our diagram uses only five biblical characters as illustrations, but this statement is true of all the men and women in the Bible who succeeded for God, and it is true of us also. Even the specific biblical references to success make it clear that success comes to us as a gift from God; it is not something we attain by ourselves.

For example, after Joseph was sold into slavery by his brothers, he rose through the ranks in Potiphar's household because "his master saw that the Lord was with him and that the Lord gave him success in everything he did" (Genesis 39:3). David, in spite of his struggles with temptation, sin, and disobedience, "in everything he did . . . had great success, because the Lord was with him" (1 Samuel 18:14).

When we choose our destination, when we set our this-is-my-heart's-desire direction, we must choose it in keeping with what we know of God's will and His commandments if we hope to succeed. Yet our inclination as human beings is to do it the other way around: We want to choose our destination and then persuade God to bless us as we pursue it. As one of my young adult Sunday school students put it, "We decide what we want to do, and then we say, 'Hey, God, back me up in this, will You?'"

To choose a destination rooted in our own desires, or in the expectations of others, or even in a worthwhile need we see in the world, is to disregard God's sovereignty. Maybe He does want us to meet that crying need in the world, or do what others have encouraged or expected us to do, or even do what we ourselves would choose if it were up to us—but our vision is too limited and our understanding too paltry to make that choice apart from His wisdom.

All Aboard!

Our journey will include these three components: Our work along the way will help shape our route; our goals will serve as milestones to check our progress; keeping our ultimate destination in mind will provide the inspiration and the vision to help us choose which turns to take and will encourage us when the road becomes narrow and rocky. What else do we need? Let's think about taking along the following.

1. An atlas.

You're on your summer vacation. The whole family is in the car and you're driving to Grand Canyon. You've spent months planning the trip, poring over the atlas as you mapped out your route. But now it's 1 A.M., and instead of being at the gates of Grand Canyon National Park as you expected, you are just entering the city limits of Feebly, Montana, population 317. Where did you go wrong?

You look at the inside front cover of the atlas. It says:

Copyright © 1971 by D. Tours, Inc. The publishers do not guarantee the accuracy of any information in this publication.

Your atlas is outdated, and some of the information in it was probably wrong to begin with. You based your whole journey on incorrect information. You wonder if you'll ever get where you're going. Your trip is ruined.

The Bible is our atlas. It's always correct and never out-of-date. To undertake our journey without it, or to use any other source as our primary guidebook, is to run the risk of ending up in the spiritual equivalent of Feebly, Montana—or worse!

2. Traveling companions.

Recently a reporter for a college alumni magazine interviewed me regarding my work as a writer. She asked, "What people in your life influenced you the most?" As I began listing individuals in answer to her question—my parents, a seventh-grade teacher, a college professor, a former employer—I realized how critical their influence in my life has been.

The men and women around us have so much to teach us. Our traveling companions can make the journey richer by sharing themselves with us, by giving us their love, affection, respect, friendship, and trust, and by allowing us to reciprocate. They can teach us from their own unique perspective, helping us learn from their experiences and maybe sparing us some painful ones of our own. They can comfort us when the traveling is tough and make us laugh when all else fails. They can challenge us to put our convictions to the test.

We need other people. If we disregard or demean the value and importance of those around us—whether family members, co-workers, friends, the server who waits on our table at the coffee shop, or the man who sits beside us on the bus—we show disrespect for what God has created. If, as we seek success, we focus only on what *we* want and need, and look at every event and situation only in terms of how it will affect *us*, we cannot fulfill God's commandment to serve Him and to serve others. I don't believe that God means for us to travel alone, or that we can achieve success in isolation.

3. Fuel.

A co-worker, Bill, and I were driving across the infamous seven-mile-long Howard Frankland Bridge that connects the cities of Tampa and St. Petersburg over Tampa Bay. We were on our way back to the office from a business appointment. Unfortunately, Bill had neglected to gas up his car before the trip, and it ran out of gas on the bridge. With no pullout lanes and no shoulders, the bridge is known throughout the area as a very hazardous place for a stalled car.

Bill got out of the car to try to flag down help. As he did so, he was hit by another car. The injuries he received crippled him for life.

Running out of fuel is dangerous. It's dangerous on a bridge, it's dangerous on the highway or on a country road, and it's dangerous as we travel along our road to success. Running out of fuel makes us vulnerable and susceptible to dangers that wouldn't otherwise threaten us. When we run out of spiritual fuel on our journey, we are less likely to be able to withstand temptation. We may choose to take the easy route instead of the right one. The compromise that seemed unthinkable before may now start to appear more attractive. Choices that seemed clear now seem muddy. Our destination starts to seem too far away, or no longer worth the effort.

How do we fuel up for this journey?

a. Prayer.

Because it is our communication with God, prayer keeps us in touch with the source of everything we need. Prayer gives us hope, confidence, assurance, and a chance to reaffirm our reliance on God. Through prayer we seek the wisdom and the strength to make right choices and to find God's will in difficult situations. Prayer relieves us of burdens by enabling us to lay them before God. Prayer gives us a channel for praise and thanksgiving when we pass milestones or travel through a stretch of beautiful country. Without prayer, our entire journey is in jeopardy.

b. The Holy Spirit.

God is at work in us through His Spirit. We can choose to listen or not to listen, to be open to His leading or not. His Spirit fuels us to do what we cannot do by ourselves: to love the unlovable, to choose the painful over the easy, to continue in the face of obstacles, to fight for good in the face of evil.

c. Rest.

My husband and I laugh about the bygone days when, as a young couple with no children, we thought nothing of jumping into our car and driving 12 or 20 or 30 hours straight for our summer vacation. We don't do that anymore. Now we drive eight or ten hours and stop. From the vantage point of middle age, we've recognized the value of rest!

We need rest on our journey toward success, too. We've all met the classic workaholic—the woman who is so consumed with her work, whether at home or on the job, that she can't focus on anything else. She takes little time out even for eating or sleeping. When she does "relax," it's only on the surface; her mind is running a mile a minute, planning the next day, making a mental to-do list, analyzing a problem. She's the first to admit that her life is out of balance, but something drives her to keep up her destructive lifestyle.

Resting on our journey doesn't mean quitting or abandoning our vision of the destination, even temporarily. It can, however, mean relaxing in the assurance that God is in control. It can mean accepting our limitations, admitting that maybe we don't need to be striving every minute to save the world or to meet everyone else's expectations (or even our own). It can mean setting aside that task we thought had to be done RIGHT NOW and taking time to regroup and renew ourselves instead. Or maybe it means savoring the most recent milestone we've passed—seeing a child off to the first day of school . . . finishing an annual report . . . completing another year of teaching Sunday school . . . rejoicing in a healed relationship. It can mean giving up the conviction that we have to be perfect or else God won't love us; it can mean abandoning the guilt-spurred belief that our families will be disappointed in us or our bosses won't promote us unless we drive ourselves relentlessly.

Jesus knew the value of rest, both physical and spiritual. He even told His disciples, "Come with me by yourselves to a quiet place and get some rest" (Mark 6:31). He offers us His rest, too.

If we fail to rest on our journey, we'll never last until the end.

We can look to other sources of fuel too. Our guide-book, the Bible, fuels us each day as we discover new insights and new applications to the circumstances and situations in our lives. Our traveling companions fuel us by the exchange of ideas, the expressions of love and caring, the unspoken support, the thumbs-up for a job well done.

We can be fueled by books that entertain or inspire us; by art, music, drama, exercise, fellowship, time alone, preaching of the gospel—by so many things. God has given us so much. If success is a process, and the journey is as important as the destination, then let's not miss any of the splendor along the way.

POINTS OF INTEREST

1. In this chapter we talked about three components of success: work, goals, and desired results. How do you think the three are related? In the space below, draw a diagram illustrating the relationship.

2. Is there a biblical character who is a special role model or inspiration to you? Using the chart below, list the route (work), the milestones (goals), and the destination (desired results) which the Bible reveals from that person's life.

Work (Route)	Goal(s) (Milestones)	Desired Results (Destination)

3. If we set a goal that we truly believe is God's will for us, but we don't reach it, have we failed? Define failure from a purely human perspective:

_____

_____

_____

What do you think is God's definition of failure?

_____

_____

4. We need the Bible as our guidebook for the journey. What other books or documents that you've read would be helpful to you personally on your journey?

_____

_____

_____

_____

_____

5. Name the five traveling companions whom you feel will influence—or have influenced—you the most on your journey toward success. Why is each of them important? How does each influence your route, your milestones, your destination, or all three?

Name   Influence

_____   _____

_____   _____

_____   _____

_____   _____

6. God makes fuel available to us on our journey, but sometimes we don't use it. What can we do to get the most mileage out of:

a) Prayer: _____

_____

b) The Holy Spirit: _____

_____

c) Rest: _____

_____

What other "fuels" are especially valuable to you, and how can you use them?

_____   _____

_____   _____

_____   _____

_____   _____

_____   _____

SIGNPOST

Be strong and very courageous. Be careful
to obey all the law my servant Moses
gave you; do not turn from it to the right
or to the left, that you may be successful
wherever you go.

—Joshua 1:7

Have faith in the LORD *your God and*
you will be upheld; have faith in his prophets
and you will be successful.

—2 Chronicles 20:20

CHAPTER 4

Wish I May, Wish I Might

Far away in the sunshine
are my highest aspirations.
I may not reach them,
but I can look up
and see their beauty,
believe in them,
and try to follow where they lead.

—Louisa May Alcott

Valerie is a young woman in her early 20's who works as a physical therapist. She described a change that occurred in her life last year.

"All of a sudden I just decided to stop dreaming and start doing things. For example, I had always dreamed of going to Europe. It was always this far-off dream, like something I'd never achieve but would always want.

"So I started looking at what it would take to make it happen, and making plans. I'm single, and I have no one to support except myself, and no one to take care of. I figured out how much the trip would cost, and how much time I would be able to take. I looked at different travel packages that would give me the most for my money—and I just went! It was the most fantastic experience of my life.

"Another thing I had been thinking about for a long time was taking an acting class. That was another dream. I thought, 'Why just dream about it? Why not do it?' So I signed up for a class at the junior college, and it was great. I'm not a very good actress, but I learned a lot in the class and enjoyed the experience.

"I'm more willing now to try to reach my goals. I've even set long-term goals—to have my own physical therapy practice within five years, and open my own clinic within ten. I want to learn more about classical music and maybe learn to play an instrument, too.

"I don't know what made the change in me, but I know that I'm excited about life now."

For Valerie, success isn't something that's reserved for other people; it's within her own reach. She has decided that she can be successful at something today and still have a goal to meet tomorrow and in the years ahead. Certainly each of us can do the same.

Making plans and setting goals help us face life with a sense of anticipation and challenge. Our goals give us those milestones we need to mark our progress along the journey.

But wait a minute. Isn't all this planning and goal-setting nonscriptural? After all, doesn't the Bible tell us to entrust our day-to-day lives to God's direction and guidance? Didn't Jesus clearly instruct us not to worry about having enough to eat or drink or wear? Didn't the biblical writer James warn us about relying on our own plans and making statements such as "Today or tomorrow we will go to this or that city, spend a year there, carry on business and make money" (James 4:13)? Aren't we undermining God's sovereignty in our lives if we make our own plans and set our own goals?

Besides, in Chapter 2 we talked about the dangers of letting goals be the sole basis of our definition of success. Are goals good or aren't they?

It sounds like we need to look more closely at this issue of planning and goal-setting if we are to continue our journey toward success. Let's explore some of the questions above.

The Best-Laid Plans...

I don't think that planning and goal-setting are non-scriptural but I do believe that we need to heed James' warning about getting too carried away with our own ideas and too locked into our own plans. Whether our goals work for us or against us as we seek God's will depends largely on two factors: 1) the balance between our reliance on God's direction and our willingness to take action on our own, and 2) the destination—the "desired results"—on which we base our goals.

Let's look first at the question of how our goals and plans are related to seeking and doing God's will.

After giving us his clear warning in verse 4:13, James goes on to give this advice: "You ought to say, 'If it is the Lord's will, we will live and do this or that' " (James 4:15). "If it is the Lord's will" is the operative phrase in that passage. We can make all the plans we want, but we must beware of crossing the line between seeking to do God's will and seeking only to meet our own desires. We honor Him when we acknowledge that anything we do is made possible only by His grace and when we earnestly try to discern His will as we make decisions and plans in our daily lives.

At the same time, I believe that God expects us to do our part to make His will happen. To say, "Lord, help me to do Your will," and then not do anything ourselves, won't make God's will happen. He gave us a will of our own, and we can use it to choose actions and make decisions that reflect His desire, at least as we understand it. We are His hands and feet in bringing about what He desires on earth. Carrying out His will is something that we do in partnership with Him; we aren't inanimate chess pieces on a cosmic board, waiting for God's hand to move us to another square. A partnership only works when both partners do their share.

My friend Cathy has a wonderful sense of this balance between relying on God's will and making her own decisions, plans, and goals. Right now she's going to college to earn a degree in education.

"I really believe God's will for me is to work with children in some way," she told me. "There are so many avenues for doing that, although right now I have no idea what specific work He has in store for me to do. For now I'm just excited about all I'm learning, and I'm looking forward to discovering what work He has for me."

Cathy's destination is to serve God through working with children. Her current goal is to complete her college education. Then she can begin to explore the various job opportunities available to her and the many kinds of work in which she can help bring God's love and His message to children.

Cathy recognizes the dangers of becoming too focused on our own goals.

"I think we have to be careful," she said, "that we don't get so wrapped up in heading toward our goals that we forget to let God use us and work in us along the way.

"Some people I know," she went on, "set a goal—like becoming a minister, for example—and they feel that God can't use them until they reach that goal.

"But He can use us at any time. I think we have to avoid getting so focused on the goal that we miss out on what's between here and there."

Cathy's comment reinforces the idea that success is a journey rather than a destination. Each day that God uses us or teaches us or enables us to know more about Him, we experience success; we don't have to reach our far-off destination or even meet a specific goal to feel successful. He gives us success all along the way as we rely on Him and grow closer to becoming the women He would have us be.

Still, that far-off destination is important. It affects the kinds of work we choose and the day-to-day lives we lead. It determines the goals we set and the things we do to meet them.

In Chapter 3 we called this our "desired result" and our destination. We can also call it a dream or a vision. It's that hoped-for, distant goal that colors everything we do. It gives an added quality of purpose and anticipation to our journey.

For one thing, *our chosen destination affects all the decisions we make along the way.*

If I have a choice between two job offers, how do I decide between the two? Obviously there are many factors, but, all other things being equal, I would want to choose the one that will help me move toward my ultimate goal, my highest aspiration. If a research biologist dreams of finding a way to make the earth feed more people, then a job with an agricultural company would be more attractive than a job in a medical laboratory.

A working mother has only so many off-the-job hours a week. (I refuse to call this "leisure time," because everyone knows it's not!) She needs to make decisions about how she will spend that time. The destination she has in view for herself and her family will dictate the choices she makes about that time.

Our choice of destination affects how we feel about ourselves.

Keeping our destination in view enables us to see ourselves as something other than what we are right now. It gives us a glimpse of our own potential, a chance to see ourselves perhaps as God sees us. By dreaming of what we will be or do someday, we reaffirm that we are capable of far more than we are able to do and be right now.

Our destination motivates us to keep moving ahead.

An elderly women who used to be my neighbor had Alzheimer's disease. Although she appeared to be in excellent health otherwise, she experienced frequent and unexpected periods of forgetfulness. It wasn't unusual for her to get in her car and head for the beauty parlor a mile away, then suddenly be unable to remember where she had intended to go. What a frightening, hopeless feeling it must have been to find herself away from home and not know where she was or why she was there!

We can experience this same disoriented feeling about our lives if we have no sense of where we intend to go. Our chosen destination, no matter how remote it might appear, gives us the motivation to keep going, to forge ahead even when there seem to be obstacles everywhere. It's the light on the horizon, the treasure at the end of the rainbow. It inspires us to continue our journey.

Our dreams give our lives a sense of purpose, so that the things we do become meaningful. Without them, life can seem either like a meaningless tangle of unrelated ups and downs or else a long, monotonous task of maintaining the status quo. Neither offers us the excitement and challenge that a well-chosen destination can provide.

What Do Potted Plants Know About Dreams?

My grandmother's kitchen in her big, country-style house was a wonderful place. One of its many fascinations for me as a young child was the long row of potted African violets along the windowsill. Sometimes she would let me carefully water them, being sure to give them just the right amount of water.

Another part of the ritual was to turn the pots around. The leaves and flowers all grew toward the sunny window, which gave the plants a leaning, windblown look, as though they were falling over. I would turn the pots so that the stems leaned away from the window, and then they would gradually straighten up as they turned back toward the light. Eventually, of course, they would once again be leaning toward the window, and I would turn the pots around again to start the process over.

Like my grandmother's violets, we too grow toward the light—the light of our fondest hopes and dreams. That's why it's so vital that we choose our destination with care and discernment. It affects our decision-making, influences our self-image, and shapes what we will become. In large measure, our destination and the goals we set to reach it direct our growth. Depending on what we hope for and aspire to, we can grow to be more like Christ and more like the child of God He designed us to be, or we can grow toward worldliness, sin, and unhappiness.

The apostle Paul confirms repeatedly that our hopes and dreams shape our spiritual growth. "I press on toward the goal to win the prize for which God has called me heavenward in Christ Jesus," he wrote (Philippians 3:14). "Do you not know that in a race all the runners run, but only one gets the prize? Run in such a way as to get the prize" (1 Corinthians 9:24).

For us to realize the potential that God created in us, we have to insure that our chosen destination is pleasing to Him and in keeping with His commandments. In Paul's letter to the Romans he encouraged believers to "offer your bodies as living sacrifices, holy and pleasing to God" (Romans 12:1). He urges us to commit all that we are—not just physically but spiritually, emotionally, and mentally—to God so that we can bring about His will.

If God called you and me today to present our dreams and aspirations before Him as part of that "living sacrifice," would we be proud to reveal to Him openly our destination and our fondest hopes? Or would they reveal us to be self-serving, greedy, materialistic, or just apathetic? Would they reflect His call to serve Him and others, or reveal that we have only our own wants and interests at heart?

The Fine Art of Goal-Setting

Our choice of destination obviously determines the nature of the goals we choose. If the ultimate result we desire from our efforts is to bring acclaim to ourselves or attain some worldly standard we've set, then our goals will reflect that. If our ultimate destination is to do the work to which God calls us, then our goals will reflect that desire. In turn, our goals will influence the work we choose.

We can learn a great deal about setting goals from the example of Solomon, who became heir to the throne of Israel at the most glorious period of his nation's history. When Solomon ascended the throne, God appeared to him and said, " 'Ask for whatever you want me to give you.'

"Solomon answered God, '. . . Give me wisdom and knowledge, that I may lead this people, for who is able to govern this great people of yours?'

"God said to Solomon, 'Since this is your heart's desire and you have not asked for wealth, riches or honor, nor for the death of your enemies, and since you have not asked for a long life but for wisdom and knowledge . . . therefore wisdom and knowledge will be given you. And I will also give you wealth, riches and honor, such as no king who was before you ever had and none after you will have'" (2 Chronicles 1:7-12).

Solomon had the opportunity to ask God for anything—*anything*! Imagine what would go through your own mind if God appeared to you with that invitation: "Ask for whatever you want me to give you." Perhaps God was testing Solomon, seeing what this young king would choose to ask of Him. Instead of asking for wealth and power and conquest, Solomon asked for wisdom and knowledge to govern God's people. He recognized his own inadequacy for the task. Because of his devotion and humility, not only did God grant Solomon's request, but He gave him "wealth, riches and honor" as well.

The "destination" Solomon set for himself was to govern God's people wisely and to honor God. The milestones on that journey, as recorded in the Bible, included:

- Being known throughout the world for his wisdom and discernment.
- Building the most magnificent temple in the world.
- Establishing commerce on a greater scale than his part of the world had seen before.

Any of these achievements could have been ends in themselves, but they were only stops on Solomon's route to succeeding in the work to which God had called him.

I believe that God puts each of us to the same test. He invites us to ask Him for what we want and need. God wants to help us meet our goals and attain our dreams, so that we can reach our full potential to be what He created us to be. The kind of requests we make reveal our hearts. They tell us a great deal about ourselves, perhaps showing us things we would rather not know.

Scripture is clear about what kind of requests God honors. First, we are to ask God to meet our spiritual needs, and then our earthly needs will follow. "Do not worry, saying, 'What shall we eat?' or 'What shall we drink?' or 'What shall we wear?' For the pagans run after these things, and your heavenly Father knows that you need them. But seek first his kingdom and his righteousness, and all these things will be given to you as well" (Matthew 6:31-33). For example, on the day we begin a new job, we might pray for God's blessing on us in this new undertaking. Which of the following prayers do you think would be more pleasing to God?

> "Lord, help me to do such a good job in this new position that I'll be promoted within six months and receive a 25 percent raise"
>
> or
>
> "Lord, allow me to perform this job in a way that will glorify You and bring honor to Your name."

There's a difference, isn't there?

Does this mean we can't hope to be promoted within six months and receive a raise? I don't think so. We can even chart a course for rising through the corporate ranks, calculate how much money we expect to make within what period of time, and plan our career and our budget accordingly.

However, such plans, and the goals built into them, can begin to interfere with our spiritual well-being if the plans become more important than pleasing God and doing His will. For example, suppose my plan calls for being promoted to supervisor and then to department head within five years. What happens if, as a supervisor, I find that my job is consuming so much of my time and energy that my family responsibilities are suffering? Or what if I find that, once I'm in a supervisory role, I'm expected to cut corners or manipulate other people in a way that doesn't square with my Christian convictions? Now I have to make a choice between meeting the goals in my plan and doing what's right in God's sight. Surely it can't be God's will for me to remain in that position and compromise my priorities or my ethical standards. It's time to seek God's wisdom and adjust the course I've set.

Secondly, we are to ask with right motives when we make requests of God. "When you ask, you do not receive, because you ask with wrong motives, that you may spend what you get on your pleasures" (James 4:3).

When we set goals that have to do with power, or wealth, or prestige, we need to be alert to the reasons we want to meet those goals. Is it our ego driving us, needing reassurance of our own worth and ability? Is it a need to prove ourselves to the world, to gain recognition so we'll feel good about ourselves? Or is it a desire to maximize the talents God has given us as a testimony to Him and in order to be as useful in His work as we can? God needs men and women of wealth, men and women of power and prestige and authority and accomplishment. But above all, He needs men and women committed to Him, whatever their circumstances.

Getting Down to Business

Let's look at some modern-day examples of how the destination we choose affects both the goals we set and the work we do.

After graduating from college, Margaret entered a career in advertising and marketing. She worked in the marketing departments of two major companies, did some freelance work, and also worked a couple of years each at two different advertising agencies.

Although Margaret enjoyed her work, she was dismayed when she realized that, as in any business, the advertising business has its share of questionable practices that are widely accepted. In one job she found herself working for a boss who was more concerned about getting the results he wanted than about the ethics of the means he used to get them. (This isn't an indictment of the advertising business; it's just a story about the real world.) It bothered her greatly to work in an environment where there was so little regard for honesty and integrity.

Eventually Margaret arrived at the point where she felt she had enough knowledge, experience, and skill to start her own advertising and marketing firm. If she were self-employed, she reasoned, she could run her business according to her own principles rather than having to follow someone else's. She quit her job at the agency and began working on her own.

After about 2½ years, though, she found herself forced to reevaluate her situation. The market for advertising services had grown intensely competitive; anyone who needed an advertising agency could find a dozen qualified to do the work. Big agencies with large staffs and hefty budgets snatched up all the best clients. Small businesses that came to her for help with their "advertising" really only wanted someone to make a sign that said "Special: donuts $3.99/dozen." Margaret reluctantly decided to start sending out resumés and go back to working for someone else instead of being her own boss.

"At first," she said, "I saw it as a failure. I hadn't been able to make a go of my own business. I hadn't been successful.

"Then I talked about it with a friend. She said, 'Why do you feel as though you've failed? Working for someone else isn't a disgrace. You still have all the talent and skill you had 2-1/2 years ago, plus you've gained a lot more experience. If anything, you're more of a success now than you were before.'

"She helped me see that I had been defining success as having my own advertising business and making a certain amount of money in a certain period of time. That wasn't even what I'd really wanted; what I wanted in the first place was to be able to do quality work with integrity and honesty. I can succeed at that in lots of job settings; I don't have to have my own firm to do it."

Margaret had lost sight of her real destination. Let's fill in the work-goals-results chart on the next page— Diagram 2—that we used in Chapter 3 and see how Margaret's experience shapes up.

What if Margaret had approached the idea of starting her own company in a whole different way, with a purely worldly destination in mind? Let's assume that her ultimate desire was to prove that a woman could make it in the competitive world of advertising. Refer to Diagram 3 to see how the chart might look then.

If Margaret chose her goals and her destination on this basis, then she would certainly consider herself a failure if her business didn't do well. Not only would she not have met her goals, but she wouldn't have reached her destination, either.

Diagram 2

	Work	Goal(s)	Desired Results
Margaret *(Version #1)*	Designing ads Identifying clients' needs Planning marketing campaigns	Establish positive relation-ships with clients and co-workers Maintain consistently high quality in my work Create an award-winning advertising campaign	Demonstrate Christian values in the advertising business Be used by God as a testimony in the business world

Diagram 3

	Work	Goals	Desired Results
Margaret (*Version #2*)	Designing ads Identifying clients' needs Planning marketing campaigns	Establish my firm as a leader in the community Do million-dollar business within five years Create an award-winning advertising campaign	Prove that a woman can make it as president of her own advertising agency

That's one of the beauties of choosing a destination that focuses on doing God's will and growing spiritually. When we meet the goals we set, we're never left with that feeling of "What do I do now?" There are always new goals to attain and new destinations to seek, because spiritual growth has no boundaries.

At the same time, if one of our goals eludes us, we haven't failed; we've just learned something. Now we need to go back to the drawing board with God and seek what else He would have us do.

Let's look at another chart, Diagram 4. This one is mine.

I have already written a book for working mothers, so perhaps I've met that particular goal. Now I can go on and set another goal, while keeping my eye on the same destination.

What if things had worked out differently? What if after I started work on my first book I found I just didn't have the ability or the interest in writing that I thought I had? Maybe I wouldn't have met that goal of writing a book, but with God's help I could surely find another goal that would enable me to progress toward my destination. I could start a support group for working women at my church or a Bible study for some of the women at work. I wouldn't be a failure just because I didn't meet my one particular goal of writing a book.

This brings up another important aspect of goal-choosing: taking stock of the gifts and talents that God gives us.

You're Such a Gifted Person!

Our work, our goals, and even our chosen destination are greatly influenced by the talents and abilities that God gives us. Unfortunately, they're also greatly influenced by our *perception* of our gifts. The problem is that sometimes our perception falls short of God's reality when it comes to evaluating our strengths and weaknesses, our talents, our aptitudes, and our special gifts.

Diagram 4

Work	Goal(s)	Desired Result
Writing	Write a book to encourage working mothers	Use my writing ability to help working women in their walk with God

Elsa

Each of us is given different resources with which to carry out the unique role that God has for us in His kingdom. He equips us with innate talent, physical capabilities, and the capacity to master new insights, skills, and information. He gives us the ability to learn from our experiences, so that as we move through life we become unique walking encyclopedias, filled with an intricate base of knowledge and experience that is ours alone.

This package of personal resources is different for each person. If we try to determine our own success on the basis of the gifts someone else has been given, it's like trying to wear someone else's clothes; it's always a poor fit.

Similarly, if we define ourselves and our abilities by some narrow standard based on our limited understanding, we can cut ourselves off from reaching the potential that God has for us. He doesn't see us as we see ourselves; He sees what we *can* do and be, not what we *have* been, or even what others *expect* us to be.

Jeanne excelled in math all through school. Her parents and teachers praised her analytical mind and lightning-fast calculations. Somewhere along the line someone said to her, "You're not much of a 'people person'; you're the kind of person who likes to tackle a difficult formula and work it through until you come up with the answer."

Jeanne majored in computer science in school, and went to work for a computer company. She's been with them three years, troubleshooting complex problems and tackling difficult programing tasks. Now, though, she feels like she would enjoy a change, perhaps going into computer software sales. She even has a friend who has offered to put her in touch with the sales manager of a well-respected software company.

Jeanne knows that having a pleasant personality and being able establish rapport with customers are essential to doing well in sales work. She thinks she could do it—but there's that voice saying, "You're not much of a people person." She wonders if she would do better to stay in her present work; maybe it's the only thing she's really cut out for.

Do you think Jeanne is defined in God's book as "Jeanne: a person who's good at math"? I don't. "Whatever work God has for you," my friend Cathy says, "He'll give you the resources to do it."

Perhaps her discontent with her present job situation is a sign that God wants Jeanne to have more contact with people, to be a testimony for Him in a different way. If she has sought His will and feels that the sales job opportunity is one He wants her to seek, then her past perception of herself as the non-people-math-whiz needs to be scrapped.

Jeanne certainly wouldn't be alone in making a move to a different kind of work. I'm excited to see how many women I know have made major changes in both the kind of work they do and the goals they've set. Their destination remains basically the same: to be Christ's ambassadors. But they've learned that in God's "Help Wanted" column, the opportunities are unlimited.

Janet was a dental hygienist. Single and without children, she now travels around the country giving motivational speeches for a national management training company. Cathy, whom I mentioned earlier, was the anchor for a Christian television program before she decided to become a teacher. Paula was the administrative assistant in an advertising agency before she became a paralegal.

This ability—or flex-ability—to see ourselves in terms of our potential rather than just our experiences also gives us more opportunity to accommodate our family responsibilities. Tina, for example, was a full-time television producer before her daughter was born; now she's a freelance publicist working out of her home. Joan was a loan officer in a bank; now she's a full-time mother who uses her administrative skills as a member of her church's governing board. Carolyn was a secretary until her second child was born and she decided to be a stay-at-home mother.

These women were willing to take a chance on themselves and on God's plan for them. They were willing to see themselves in a new way, exploring the gifts He had given them in a different setting.

Our perception of ourselves is limited, but God's isn't. He sees an unlimited number of avenues through which we can use our gifts to be successful for Him. When we choose a destination that keeps us reliant on His will and open to His guidance, our work can change, and our goals can change, our dreams and hopes can change, but we're still destined for success.

I can hear you saying, "But I don't have any special talents. I'm just an ordinary person." Problem: God doesn't make ordinary people. He makes only unique and special people, because that's His design.

This feeling that we are "ordinary" if we don't have a brilliant musical talent or a flamboyant, artistic streak stems from our misunderstanding of the talents God gives. This misunderstanding leads us to define success in terms of the world's popular definition instead of one that's in keeping with God's design. We begin to think that He gives gifts and talents to only select people, and that the rest of us are just assembly-line creations He stamps out of a mold. That's not how the Bible describes it.

> You created my inmost being; You knit me together in my mother's womb. I praise you because I am fearfully and wonderfully made.
>
> —Psalm 139:13,14

Does that sound like the creation of a run-of-the-mill creature? God gives loving attention to the creation of each human being, equipping that person for a one-of-a-kind role in His kingdom, and then giving us the choice of whether we will fulfill that role or not. The gifts and talents that God chooses to give us represent a part of that loving creation.

The apostle Paul explained in his letters how the church is made up of different people contributing their different gifts to the good of the whole:

"Just as each of us has one body with many members, and these members do not all have the same function, so in Christ we who are many form one body, and each member belongs to all the others. We have different gifts, according to the grace given us" (Romans 12:4-6).

We are supposed to be different from one another. We're like snowflakes—distinctive! God's plan for us is unique because we are uniquely equipped to carry it out—and vice versa.

When I reflect on the nature of God's special gifts to people, I often think of my friend Paula. She's been "successful" in the traditional job sense during her career in business. She's extremely intelligent, efficient, well-organized, and skilled at working with other people.

When Paula and I worked for the same company many years ago, it soon became evident to me that she had been given another gift, too: the gift of encouragement. Paula's spirit is so generous and compassionate that just being around her is encouraging. She genuinely cares about people, and as a result she's the one whom co-workers invariably seek out when they have a problem. They know they can count on Paula to listen with real concern and a sincere desire to help.

Several months ago the building in which I worked was destroyed by fire. It was a beautiful, brand-new building that the hospice I work for had bought with contributions from the people of our community. We had moved in just seven months earlier, and were enjoying the excitement of being in our new office home. And then, early one morning when the building was empty, fire destroyed it completely.

Although we were thankful that no one had been hurt, we felt like we had experienced a death. Our long-awaited "home" was gone. Many of our staff worked around the clock just to keep the agency's programs operating. The strain of working without a workplace was tremendous. We crowded into borrowed office space nearby, with dozens of staff members sharing inadequate work space, a very few telephones, virtually no supplies or materials, no files, no records—not much of anything.

A few days later I received a card from Paula saying, "I heard about the fire. I know this must be a very hard time for you. I just want you to know I'm thinking of you. Call me if you need a friend."

Most people saw the television and newspaper accounts the day after the fire and forgot about it. Paula, though, with her special gift, saw that I would need some encouragement at that later time.

Is there someone you know who has that special gift of encouragement? What are your gifts?

How each of us will define success for ourselves must surely be rooted in these special gifts that God has chosen to give us. He has equipped us in this unique way for a purpose, and if we are to "succeed," then part of that success must be to use our gifts as He desires.

God knows us better than we know ourselves. When we set our sights and make our plans, we do so based on the infinitesimally small amount of self-knowledge and wisdom that we have. Maybe we'll make some right choices and right plans, and maybe we won't. But when we rely on *God's* guidance, and base our plans on *His* Word and *His* will, then we are assured of finding the best possible course for our journey.

I Must Be Dreaming

I believe that God wants us to dream of doing great things for Him, and I believe He wants us to do them, too. I believe He wants us to be infinitely successful as women of faith, courage, and strength. He is a great God. He sees capabilities and possibilities that we cannot see. I don't believe He wants us to limit ourselves by narrow thinking, by setting limitations on what we believe we can do and be.

The circumstances of our lives might be discouraging. We might look to the future with a sense of hopelessness or despair. We may not be able to see how a situation or relationship can ever be resolved or improved. But God sees. He can change us and He can enable us to change the things around us.

Yet our dreams must center on His will. For us to dream of greatness apart from Him is to dream of emptiness. Without Him, and without the example and salvation of Christ, there is no greatness in us. Our success begins with His graciousness. From there it's a glorious partnership, a side-by-side journey of exploration, discovery, and growth.

As we work toward a new definition of success, part of the preparation for our journey is revisiting those recesses of our hearts where we store up our most precious dreams. Maybe we need to choose a new destination.

I believe that God's hope for us is to know Him, to walk ever more closely with Him, and ultimately to be reunited with Him. When our dream, our chosen destination, is in keeping with His dream for us, success is not only a possibility but a daily reality.

In the next three chapters we'll look at how the work we do is related to the goals and destinations we've chosen, and vice versa.

POINTS OF INTEREST

1. Some people find planning and goal-setting helpful and encouraging; others prefer to live day to day without a lot of thought for the future. Which kind of personality are you?

_____ I carefully plan everything I do.

_____ I make plans sometimes, but not always.

_____ I only make plans for activities like having a party or going on a trip; I don't chart the course of my life.

_____ I don't plan much of anything unless it's absolutely necessary.

2. List the benefits and the dangers of goal-setting and planning as we've discussed in this chapter.

Benefits   Dangers

_____   _____

_____   _____

_____   _____

_____   _____

_____   _____

_____   _____

3. Remember when God told Solomon to ask Him for whatever He wanted? Given the same opportunity, what would you ask for?

_____

_____

4. James talks about the motives that prompt us to ask for things from God. For each request you listed above, identify your motivation for asking God for it.

_____

_____

_____

_____

_____

5. What special gifts has God given you? List them below. Besides gifts like mathematical ability or musical talent, consider gifts like encouragement, insight, empathy, sensitivity, perceptiveness, etc. Don't be modest!

_____

_____

_____

_____

_____

_____

_____

6. What are some things you can do this week to use these gifts in a way that will be a testimony to your Christian faith? How are these gifts related to your goals and dreams?

_____

_____

_____

_____

_____

There are different kinds of gifts,
but the same Spirit.
There are different kinds of service,
but the same Lord.
There are different kinds of working,
but the same God
works all of them in all men.

—1 Corinthians 12:4-6

Remain in me, and I will remain in you.
No branch can bear fruit by itself;
it must remain in the vine.
Neither can you bear fruit
unless you remain in me.

—John 15:4

Now to him who is able to do immeasurably
more than all we ask or imagine, according
to his power that is at work within us,
to him be glory in the church and in Christ
Jesus throughout all generations,
for ever and ever!

—Ephesians 3:20,21

PART TWO

Work—
Baggage or Blessing?

CHAPTER 5

Making Work Work

*To love what you do
and feel that it matters—
how could anything be more fun?*

—Katherine Graham

Do you listen to the radio on your way home from work? I do.

One radio station I used to listen to in another part of the country had a special name for that late-afternoon rush-hour period when people are headed home. They called it "Happy Go-Home Time."

A radio station here in town has a factory whistle that their DJ's blast over the airwaves at 5 P.M. to celebrate the end of the workday. The whistle is accompanied by cheers, clapping, and the sound of party horns. The station always plays fast-paced, lively songs to add to the going-home festivities.

Why is it that leaving work at the end of the day is such cause for celebration? What does that tell us about the way we feel about our work? Sometimes conversations in the break room or employee lounge give the impression that getting off work at the end of the day is akin to being let out of prison. Do we really hate our work so much that all we want is for quitting time to arrive?

I think our society is pervaded by a love-hate relationship with work. All of us, at one time or another, probably view it as a necessary nuisance, something we have to do to make ends meet financially. At other times we feel blessed by it, challenged by it, and rewarded intellectually or creatively or emotionally by it. At still other times we don't give it much thought; we just do it. Our feelings about work seem to run the gamut from one extreme to the other.

As we seek a godly standard for success, our feelings about our work will play an important role in that standard. If we're to arrive at a usable concept of success, we'll have to make some decisions about the role of work in our lives.

What Am I Doing Here?

Sociologists and psychologists who study today's work force tell us that many people are no longer content simply to receive a paycheck for their work; they want to receive nonmonetary benefits from it as well. They want to derive satisfaction from their work and to feel that it has value to the organization they work for. They want opportunities for growth and advancement. They want a sense of security and of participation in the important decisions that affect their livelihood. All these things can influence how a person feels about her work. Mothers working at home raising families, including those without outside employment, want to feel that their work is valued and appreciated in their households.

Recent news stories reporting the results of these studies and surveys make it sound as though this desire to be happy in our work were a discovery of modern research. In reality, it isn't new. The biblical writer of Ecclesiastes, contemplating life as he knew it long ago, recognized that being happy in our work is part of our overall satisfaction with life.

"My heart took delight in all my work, and this was the reward for all my labor" (2:10b).

"Moreover, when God gives any man wealth and possessions, and enables him to enjoy them, to accept his lot and be happy in his work—this is a gift of God" (5:19).

What does it take for us to be "happy in our work"?

Before we answer that question, let's do a quick survey to see what your feelings are about your work.

1. When you're at work, do you feel—
   a) Happy to be there?
   b) Okay about being there, as long as you don't have to stay too long?
   c) Like you'd rather be somewhere else?
   d) Like you'd rather be *anywhere* else?

2. Would you rather have the chicken pox than go to work?

3. When you're at work, do you feel that if you suddenly disappeared, no one would notice except the man who services the coffee machine?

4. Do you favor legislation abolishing the 40-hour workweek in favor of a 14-hour one?

5. In order to regulate agricultural prices, the government often pays farmers for *not* growing crops in their fields. Would you support economic measures in which you would get paid for *not* going to work?

6. Do you refer to your day(s) off as "a little taste of paradise"?

7. At quitting time, do you find yourself humming the *Hallelujah Chorus?*

8. Would you describe your work as:
   a) Satisfying most of the time?
   b) Satisfying part of the time?
   c) Unrewarding?
   d) Slightly better than having a root canal?

9. When you are at work, does time seem to—
   a) Fly by?
   b) Pass fairly fast?
   c) Go fast at some times and drag at others?
   d) Be going backwards?

10. If someone told you your company was closing down and you would have to find another job, but the company would pay you until you found one, would you say:
   a) "No! Please! Don't take away my job. Just let me keep doing it—you don't have to pay me. I'll do it free!"
   b) "But I like this job. I'll miss it."
   c) "A job is a job; one's no different from another."
   d) "This is a good chance to try something new."
   e) "I'm dreaming; I know I'm dreaming. This is too good to be true."

Now that you've had a chance to reflect on your feelings about your work, let's go back to the question of what it takes for us to be happy in our work. Business analysts have identified what they think are important factors; their list includes things like opportunities for advancement, benefits such as insurance, sick leave, and vacation, performance incentives, etc. While those certainly may be important, I believe that real meaning and satisfaction in work come from within us, rather than from programs or policies our employer offers.

The Big Picture

When I was in Atlanta for a convention last summer, I became acquainted with a cab driver named Harold. Cheerful and outgoing, he chatted amiably as he drove me around the city. He told me proudly that he had his own small cab company, and that his company had been selected to provide all cab services for a major international corporation that had its headquarters there in Atlanta. He had several other drivers working for him, and anytime that company needed a cab, they would call him and he would provide the service.

"I'm not just a cab driver, you see," he said. "I'm in the transportation business.

"You have to take pride in what you do if you want to get ahead," he went on. "You've got to provide good service to people. You need to treat them right, be nice to them. I keep my cabs clean and always keep the air-conditioning on in the summer and the heater on in the winter. People want to be comfortable. They're traveling, they're tired. I think,'Now what would I want if I were riding in a cab?' So I try to make them as comfortable as I can, and be nice to them, and that's how I do business."

Harold saw beyond the day-to-day task of driving a cab. He saw "the big picture": that driving a cab is providing the important service of transportation. His goal was to provide that service in the very best way possible.

I've ridden with other cab drivers who spent the whole trip complaining about everything from the weather and the government to the way their customers treated them. What a contrast with Harold's positive and optimistic outlook!

We all have bad days, and no job is enjoyable all the time. But when we can look beyond the tasks we do, whatever they are, and see a bigger picture, then we are better able to see the meaning in our work.

I believe this "bigger picture" has two dimensions, an earthly one and a spiritual one.

A few years ago, when I was managing the public-relations department of a local college, I was talking with a young woman who had started work in the department a week earlier. I had asked her, as her first assignment, to take some time to talk with each of the other staff members, so that she would have a picture of how the department worked and how each person's job contributed to the whole.

"Well," I said, "now that you've had a chance to learn about the work of the department, do you have any specific questions?"

"Yes," she said, "there's one thing I still don't quite understand."

"What's that?" I asked her.

"What do *you* do?"

I still laugh when I think about that. Her question definitely caught me off guard. After all, I was the department head! Didn't *everybody* know what I did? As I thought about it, though, I realized that while the work of other people in the department was easily seen—such as the brochures and catalogs that our graphic artist created—mine was much harder to see.

Finally I said, "Here's what I do," and I pointed to the overflowing in-basket on my desk. "I move papers from there"—and then I pointed to the out-basket—"to there."

I admit my answer was given tongue in cheek, and I did go on to explain my job more specifically, but the young woman's question had given me food for thought. If, in doing my job, I focused solely on the actual tasks—much of which really did involve handling the huge number of papers from my in-basket—then it would seem tedious indeed. I would have felt like a cog in a paperwork mill. Yet I never felt that way, because I knew that all those papers actually contributed to the operation of the college. I knew I played a small role in helping people receive an education and benefit from the opportunities it opened to them. As Harold might have put it, I wasn't just a paper-shuffler; I was in the education business.

Everyone's job is important to the organization he or she works for, or else the job wouldn't exist. If the people on the loading dock didn't load and unload the products, no one would be able to buy them. If the clerks in the billing department didn't process the invoices, bills wouldn't get paid, the company would run out of money, and there would be no paychecks. If the receptionist just stopped answering the telephone, business would soon screech to a halt. If the person who writes advertisements stopped writing them, you and I wouldn't know about new products or services that can make our lives better.

Let's look at the "big picture" of your job. Make a list of all the people who are affected by what you do. Use your imagination and think what would happen if you just stopped doing your job—even for a day. You'll see how the work you do affects numerous other people; you can picture yourself as being at the center of a set of concentric circles, each one encompassing a larger group that is affected by what you do. That's one aspect of the "big picture."

Who's Really the Boss?

If we are to incorporate the meaning of work into our definition of success, we have to be able to look past our routine day-to-day tasks and see our work on a broader scale. Success is surely something bigger than completing a day's filing or a month's worth of accounts.

Does God really care about our work? Of course He does. It's part of His "big picture" for our lives. When Paul instructs us to offer ourselves to God as "living sacrifices," this includes every hour of our day and every task we do, and this means our work is a part of that gift to God. What role does God intend for work to play in our lives?

1. God created work as an aspect of human existence.

> God blessed the seventh day and made it holy, because on it he rested from all the work of creating that he had done.
>
> —Genesis 2:3

Our world began with an act of work: creation. In those earliest days, God established work and rest as elements of our lives. Like all the things in our world, work and rest are neither good nor evil in themselves; it is *what we make of them* that makes them tools of righteousness or of evil. People who write Christian books and people who write pornographic books are both working at the same occupation—writing—but the nature and the results of their work are very different.

Similarly, resting to renew our minds and bodies is essential to a healthy lifestyle. By contrast, avoiding work out of laziness or selfishness is "rest" of a very different nature.

Whether we work outside the home or not, work is unquestionably a part of our lives. As such, we cannot ignore it as we seek to determine and to carry out God's plan for us.

2. Work gives us additional opportunities to exercise the gifts and resources God has given us.

Lisa is an accountant. She has a talent for unraveling complex transactions, organizing other people's haphazard financial records, and helping people to make the most of their money.

Susan is a landscaper. She helps people decide what their yard needs for the appearance they want, and then she does the work to make that happen. She's knowledgeable about plants and skilled at knowing how best to arrange and care for them.

Jackie is an organizer. A busy volunteer, she can organize a glittering fund-raising dinner or a neighborhood crime-prevention program that will run like clockwork. She has the gift of administration—seeing how to get things done and then doing what it takes.

These individuals' work gives them the opportunity to use the innate talents and gifts that God has given them, along with the skill, knowledge, and experience He has enabled them to obtain along the way.

What opportunities does your job provide for you to exercise your special gifts? Perhaps your present work is directly related to them, or perhaps not. Either way, work is a good place to put those gifts into action.

3. *Work provides a context for learning and spiritual growth.*

I think that the workplace, whatever kind of work we do, is an excellent training ground for Christian maturity. It gives us a chance, in a setting other than our homes, to put into action the values Christ taught us and the example He gave us. When we feel that a supervisor has treated us unfairly, we can ask ourselves, "What would Christ do in this situation?" When a co-worker's unkind remark hurts us, we can choose a response that will be pleasing to God instead of lashing out in anger. When a friend's emergency at home makes her fall behind in her work, we can practice compassion and servanthood as we look for ways to help.

Specifically, work can help us grow in several areas.

• *Discipline.* This is one of those facets of Christian life that's like cough medicine. You know you need it, but it's tough to take. A work setting provides lots of opportunities for learning to be more disciplined. Unfortunately, for me just getting up at 6:15 A.M. requires discipline, but the work setting fosters discipline in other ways, too: making the best possible use of the time and skill that God gives us for each workday; constantly striving to produce the best work we can instead of just meeting the minimum standard to get the job done; respecting our employer's time, money, property, and authority when other demands compete for our attention. All these things require discipline, and each day offers us ample opportunities for practicing it.

• *Self-control.* The workplace—as well as volunteer work—gives us an abundance of opportunities to practice self-control. Here are some "practice exercises" which the average work situation might offer.

It's 4:45 P.M. You've had a hectic day and you have a mental list of ten errands you need to do on your way home. The boss stops by your desk and says, "I need these information packets pulled together for tonight's meeting. I really need you to do it before you leave." You're tempted to mutter or gripe to your friend at the next desk—but you don't.

Your co-worker, Janie, calls in sick, and all her work ends up on your desk. The next day she tells you confidentially, "I wasn't really sick. My friend Sue was here from out of town and she wanted to spend the day at the beach, so I decided to go with her." You can't believe she could have been so irresponsible, and you consider making an unkind remark—but you don't.

The table at lunch is buzzing with gossip about the attractive new clerk in payroll and the accounting supervisor who's separated from his wife. You're very tempted to toss in your two cents' worth of speculation about what might be going on, because, after all, you *did* hear a rumor from someone who's right there in the accounting department—but you keep quiet and try to change the subject.

Your son is doing an art project, and the advertising department at work has drawers full of colored markers just like he needs. Your friend who works in that department says, "Why don't you come by and just take a handful? They have zillions of them. Who's to know?" But you stop on the way home and buy a box of markers instead.

"The fruit of the Spirit is . . . self-control" (Galatians 5:22,23).

• *Patience and forgiveness.* God has made each person unique. Our experiences, background, family situations, value systems, and personalities all affect the way we are. Because we're all different, each of us is able to get along better with some types of people than others, and we usually choose to associate with people with whom we have basic interests, traits, and values in common. Even within our circle of friends, misunderstandings and disagreements can arise.

In a work situation, though, we're likely to spend a great deal of time with people very different from us, people with whom we wouldn't choose to spend that much time if it were up to us. Under the pressures and forced togetherness of the workplace, the differences between people can give rise to tension and conflict that ultimately produce hurt feelings, anger, and strained or damaged relationships. What a perfect setting for learning patience and forgiveness!

Christ's loving acceptance of us in spite of our sins and spiritual shortcomings is our model for dealing with those around us: the person whose sarcastic humor is hurtful instead of funny; the boss who always has to find someone to blame—other than herself—when things go wrong; the co-worker who tries to take credit for your ideas; the abrupt, unfriendly supervisor who can't seem to cooperate with anyone else.

Christ has shown us how we are to relate to others. It's as important to follow His example in our workplaces as in our homes or our churches.

• *Decision-making.* Our work opens up a whole new crop of decisions to be made. The fundamental decision about what role work will play in our lives, and how it will be related to our definition of success, is one of the most important among all those decisions. Others relate to day-to-day ethical choices about responsibility to our employer versus our own desires, needs, or spiritual values; respect for authority; and honesty and integrity in the conducting of business. Then there is another whole set of decisions relating to job and career choices, money, and the balance between work and other aspects of our lives. Every day our work presents us with choices between what God would have us do and what human nature dictates.

• *Teamwork.* In the last chapter we talked about the way God equips us uniquely to do the work He has designed for us in His kingdom. In this vein, the apostle Paul compares the church to the human body, made up of many parts, each one of which is important even though they are all so different. Each part is dependent on the others.

The workplace is like that. We have to work together to accomplish what our department or our company is supposed to do. In the workplace we have a chance to practice teamwork, combining each person's special gifts and talents to carry out the work of the group, so that the whole is indeed greater than the sum of its parts. In God's kingdom our task is the same: to combine countless individual gifts into a great work for Him.

Teamwork also helps us learn to value the contributions of others. Sometimes we think that our own gifts or skills or jobs are more important than those of other people. This is the same problem that the Corinthian church had. Some members had begun to think they were better Christians or more spiritual-minded than others because they had certain gifts. The apostle Paul made it clear that God calls us to different but equally valuable roles, and that only when we work together can His work be done.

• *Stewardship.* In many ways, our work gives us the chance to demonstrate that we can be good stewards of the things God entrusts to us, including time, gifts, knowledge, physical ability, money, authority, and leadership. Seeking to be worthy of this trust is an important facet of our spiritual growth.

"Whoever can be trusted with very little can also be trusted with much, and whoever is dishonest with very little will also be dishonest with much. So if you have not been trustworthy in handling worldly wealth, who will trust you with true riches? And if you have not been trustworthy with someone else's property, who will give you property of your own?" (Luke 16:10-12).

Till Death Do Us Part?

Let's talk some more about the issue of being happy in our work. Compatibility of our personalities, desires, values, and abilities with the work we do is a critical factor in how we feel about our jobs. As a result, the match between a person and his or her job is much like a marriage: If it's a bad match, no one is happy.

Think about it: What circumstances cause marriages to break down, and what circumstances cause job situations to deteriorate?

Unfaithfulness is one cause. It means that the two parties haven't been true to each other; they've betrayed each other's trust. The consequences of unfaithfulness in marriage are well-known, but it can happen in an employee-job relationship as well. The job can betray the employee's trust if the employer doesn't fulfill the promises that were made when the employee was hired—promises of a raise after the first year, or additional benefits, or opportunities for advancement. By the same token, it can be the employee who is "unfaithful." This can take the form of stealing from the employer by wasting the company's time or money, criticizing the employer to others, abusing privileges, betraying trust, or simply losing interest in performing the job well.

Lack of communication is another reason that human relationships deteriorate. I've heard many divorced men and women alike say that their marriages deteriorated because the spouses both grew and changed over the years, but they failed to communicate well enough to be aware of the changes in the other person. Then, when they finally realized what was happening, too much damage had occurred for them to reestablish their relationship.

The same thing can happen in a job situation: A company's management or a person's own supervisor fails to keep the person informed about what is going on or what is expected of her. One woman I know, who was the head of a hospital's public-relations department, walked into her office one Monday morning to find that the department had been abolished and that she no longer had a job. Communication had obviously broken down somewhere in a major way!

We as employees often fail to communicate, too. We may feel that work is being dumped on us without any regard for the amount of time it takes, but instead of asking our supervisor to set some priorities for us, we keep silent until we're so overwhelmed and frustrated that we begin to dread going to work. If a change in policy or personnel affects us negatively, we may just let our unhappiness fester into chronic resentment instead of asking about the change and trying to understand why it was made. The result of this failure to communicate is generally one of two things: chronic unhappiness with our job, or a "divorce" from it.

Some marriages—whether between spouses or between employees and their jobs—are just a bad match from the outset. Human beings, when they rely on their own wisdom, often make unwise decisions, and our collective batting average in choosing life-partners and jobs isn't much better than in other areas of our lives. Sometimes, even when we try hard to make a job match succeed, it just doesn't work over the long term.

Marti is a classic people-person. Outgoing, cheerful, and talkative, she thrives on meeting new people and learning what makes them tick. She's one of those individuals who can sit next to fellow passengers on a bus for ten minutes and by the end of the trip they will have told her their whole life stories!

Marti tried working as an invoice clerk for a while. Guess what—it didn't work! It was a poor match from the beginning, because she was soon starved for outside contact, and she found it hard to concentrate on the detailed, structured work that her job entailed.

Work occupies a great deal of our time. If we had the choice, would we spend all that time doing something we really didn't like? Yet many of us do just that. We remain in jobs we dislike rather than looking for something that would make us happier.

My friend Jody calls this the "Remain-and-Complain School of Employment." If we spend eight hours or so a day on the job being unhappy, we cannot escape the fact that it will eventually affect our whole outlook on life as well as our physical and emotional health. We cannot see ourselves as successful, or even potentially successful, when we feel locked into a job we dislike. We look to the future and see a dead end rather than growth or opportunity or challenge. When that happens, we inevitably find ourselves complaining constantly to anyone who will listen. Our negative feelings about work color our feelings about other areas of our lives, and we find that nothing seems to be right. We gradually succumb to a chronic unhappiness and a pervasive sense of failure and disappointment. Is that the kind of life we want?

Granted, there are times when financial considerations, geographic limitations, or other factors make it essential for us to stay in a job we really don't like at all. In that case it's up to us to seek God's help in making the best of the situation and His wisdom in dealing with it while seeking a change.

Much of the time, though, we have more choices than we think. We may stay in jobs we dislike because we lack the self-confidence to attempt a change, or because we're unwilling to take the risk of trying something new. Maybe our self-image has become so limited that we can't see ourselves in a different light: as women of ability, possessing special gifts given to us by God.

The psalmist tells us that God "watches all who live on earth" and "considers everything they do" (Psalm 33:14,15). Surely He is interested in the choices we make about work! If we find ourselves in a "bad marriage" to a job, we can rely on Him for help just as we can in other areas of our lives. Here are some steps that we can take as we seek His guidance.

1. *Pray about the job situation.*

God knows what we need before we ask Him, but He still wants us to ask. Turning over the difficulties of our job to Him gives us the assurance and the confidence that change is possible. It gives us hope and encouragement.

Being persistent in prayer is important. To ask God in one quick prayer to help you change your job situation, and then forgetting about it, is treating Him like the drive-up window at Hamburger Heaven. God deserves better treatment than that. The Bible tells us He rewards persistence and faithfulness in prayer.

2. *Do your part.*

When we ask God for help, He expects us to use the intelligence, skill, and capabilities He has given us as we work *with Him* to solve problems. We enter a partnership with Him. Our part is to explore our job options, do some serious thinking about what kind of change we want to make, and take action to pursue other opportunities He may present to us—while continuing in prayer. Under His guidance we can come to realize what is really needed. Maybe it's a change in our outlook that will solve the problem, not a change of jobs. Maybe clearing the air with a supervisor or co-worker will make a big difference in the way we feel about the situation. Maybe changing departments or changing companies is what we need.

There's always a chance, too, that God is calling us to an entirely different field of work, for which we need to obtain new training or education, or even to a different lifestyle altogether. If we have children, perhaps His desire for us is to postpone our job pursuits for a while in favor of devoting more time to our family responsibilities. If we feel strongly that a change in our work situation is needed, we need to consider that possibility, even though we might receive little support from others.

God sees options for us that we don't see, because He views our lives from a divine perspective that our limited vision cannot even begin to approach. When we entrust our job decisions to Him, we can be assured of the best possible outcome when we remain fully open to His direction.

Our human tendency, though, is to present our request to God in the form of a multiple-choice question. We identify what we think are the best options and then ask God to choose one: Option A, Option B, or Option C. When we seek His guidance by this method, we are attempting to impose our will on Him rather than seeking His for us. From what we know of God, it stands to reason that He does not welcome our attempts to manipulate Him!

3. Be patient.

Some years ago, when I realized that my job situation wasn't working out (for a variety of reasons), I began to pray that God would show me what to do. Nothing happened for months. I kept praying. Nothing happened.

As time went by, though, I grew more and more confident that something *was* going to happen. I was able to face the difficulties of my job with more optimism and more inner peace because I had the assurance that God was in control. My role during the "waiting period" was to be patient, to continue praying, and to pursue the options around me.

It took a year. At the end of that year I was in a job situation that was much better suited to my life and my priorities at that time. When I had first begun praying about a change, I never envisioned that it would turn out that way, because I didn't see all the options. But God did.

Think back to our discussion at the beginning of this chapter about our love-hate relationship with work. If the "hate" part seems to be more prevalent in your job situation than the love part, maybe you need to ask God for insight and direction about the changes you can make—in yourself and/or in your job. He wants you to be successful—by His standards—and your work can be a part of that success. Let Him take charge. After all, He created work, and He created you. Who can better help you work out the perfect "marriage" between the two?

POINTS OF INTEREST

1. On an average day, what are your feelings about your work? Where would you position yourself on the scale below?

```
_____/_____/_____/_____/_____
```
I enjoy my work   I dislike my work
most of the time   most of the time

2. Which of your gifts and abilities are reflected in the work you do?

_____

_____

_____

3. Do you have talents or capabilities that don't get used in your job as much as you would like? If so, what are they?

_____

_____

4. What do you think God would have you do with those gifts?

_____

_____

5. We discussed some opportunities for spiritual growth that work can provide. Specifically, what have you learned from your work experiences about the following aspects of Christian living?

Discipline _____

Self-control _____

Discipline _____

Self-control _____

Compassion and forgiveness _____

Decision-making _____

Servanthood _____

Teamwork _____

Stewardship _____

6. If you feel that change in your job situation is needed, and want to seek God's help in that change, the first step is to ask Him. Complete the prayer below that expresses your need to Him. Commit to praying that prayer at least once a day until the change has come about.

"Lord, thank You for Your promise to meet our needs. I want to enter into a partnership with You to change my job situation.

_____

_____ Amen."

SIGNPOST

May the favor of the Lord our God
rest upon us;
Establish the work of our hands for us—
yes, establish the work of our hands.

—Psalm 90:17

CHAPTER 6

Caution: Danger Zone

*Every job is a self-portrait
of the person who did it.*

—Source unknown

Linda enjoys her work as a corporate account repre-
sentative for an insurance company. She works
with large firms to develop and carry out employee
benefit programs such as tax-deferred annuities, pension plans, and health insurance. She takes pride in the
level of responsibility she's attained; she began with the
company three years ago as an administrative assistant,
went to college part-time, and eventually moved up to
her present position.

Linda and her husband, Rod, have two children.
When she found out she was pregnant the second time,
it was a surprise; both she and Rod had to admit it wasn't
what they wanted at that time. Linda is not very confident about her skills as a mother. She never babysat as a
child or had younger brothers and sisters, so she was
never around children much until she had her own.

Deep down, she doesn't think she's a very good

mother. She loses her temper easily with the children, especially at the end of a long workday. She feels helpless and uncertain when they're having trouble in school or they come down with one of those vague childhood flu bugs. She constantly struggles with whether to be lenient or strict, whether to be a pal to her children or to insist on their respect and obedience She loves them, but she can't seem to find ways to tell them that. Instead, it seems like most of the time that she's home—which isn't all that much—she's yelling at them and they're crying.

Her work, on the other hand, grows more and more rewarding. She loves meeting new clients and advising them about the best combination of benefits for their employees. Seeing her plans put into effect gives her a sense of satisfaction and accomplishment. Several of her clients have written glowing letters to her regional manager, praising the professional advice and conscientious service she gives them.

A regional account supervisor's job is opening up soon, and Linda is thinking of applying for it. It would involve traveling throughout the state, which would mean she would have even less time at home than she has now. Tomorrow is the deadline to apply for the new position.

If you were Linda, what would you do?

Linda's situation typifies one of the pitfalls which those of us who work outside the home need to recognize: *using work as an escape from our other responsibilities.*

Being a mother is hard. In fact, it's the hardest job that most of us will ever have. Being a faithful, loving, supportive wife can be hard, too. Fulfilling our responsibilities to our parents, our in-laws, our siblings, our churches, and our community can be difficult as well. When any of these responsibilities feels like more than we can handle, or when they turn into a constant struggle, it can make our work seem easy, satisfying, and peaceful by contrast. When that happens, we face the temptation of moving work to a higher spot on our list of priorities. We're tempted to invest a disproportionate amount of our time, energy, and effort in it simply because the rewards are more immediate and less difficult to attain than the greater rewards of family and community life.

Julia, a woman with whom I work, was experiencing a difficult time at home with her son, who was doing very poorly in school and was diagnosed as having a severe learning disability. He had become withdrawn and sullen and had begun making remarks about being a "dummy" and a "loser." Julia and her husband were trying frantically to find an educational program to help their son, and at the same time trying to restore his self-image.

"It feels so good to come to work," she told me in the middle of this period. "At least I can stop thinking about my own problems for a while."

I imagine all of us who have families and work outside the home feel this way from time to time; I know I have. Compared to the uncertainties and constant dilemmas of parenthood, our work can seem wonderfully predictable and even relaxing. I don't believe it's sinful to occasionally savor the respite it provides from the strain of family responsibilities.

Yet those responsibilities remain our first commitment, and if we begin to use our work as an excuse to avoid meeting the other demands in our lives, then I believe we are using it for the wrong purpose—tempting as it is. When we elect to give our work priority over our commitment to our families, to our churches, to our personal spiritual walk, and to the needy people of our communities, then it's time to reevaluate the role of work in our lives. We need to recheck our goals and our destination.

In the last chapter we looked at some of the ways work can benefit us in our Christian growth and in our pursuit of success that will be pleasing to God. We also need to be alert to the dangers of letting work play a role in our lives that will hinder us from attaining the success He wants for us.

How Do You Measure What a Person Is Worth?

Connie, a single mother, is a fifth-grade teacher. About halfway through the summer she became ill, and her doctor ordered her to stay in bed for three months. During that time her self-image dropped lower and lower as she spent week after week in boredom and discomfort, doing virtually nothing. It hit an all-time low when school started in the fall, since her fellow teachers were all returning to their classrooms but she wasn't. In fact, she wasn't doing anything except lying in bed, reading books and watching television. Her mother and her neighbors had to come in and prepare meals for her and her kids because she wasn't allowed to be that active.

"I finally realized," Connie said later, "that all my self-worth was tied up with my work. If I couldn't go and teach those children and run my classroom, then I felt worthless. I had to do some serious thinking about my own value as a human being. What if I was never able to teach again? If that was the only important thing in my life, then I would just die if I lost it; I wouldn't have any reason to live.

"I don't want to be like that. I don't want to depend on teaching to convince me I'm worthwhile. God has a lot invested in me, and whether I'm able to continue teaching or not, He still loves me. My worth as a person doesn't have anything to do with my job; teaching is just something God has enabled me to do to serve Him. If I can't do that any longer, I'll still matter to Him."

Connie's illness gave her an opportunity to learn something about her relationship with her work: She was using teaching to affirm her own importance in the world. Before her illness she had felt important and valuable only when she defined herself as a teacher. As a result of her illness she was able to separate her work from her identity as a person, and to see that while both are valuable, her identity doesn't have to depend on her teaching job.

How about you? If you are one of those fortunate people who has work that she loves, could you handle being unable to continue that work? What effect would that have on your feelings about yourself? About God?

Our work does not define us; *God* defines us. We are His children, and that's all the identity we need to be successful in His eyes. Keeping our spiritual destination in mind can help us maintain a balanced perspective about work and our work-related goals.

Worshiping at the Temple of Work

Do you worship your work?

Okay, you can stop laughing. If I asked you that question, you would probably picture a cartoon of yourself reverently bowing down in front of your desk or standing with a hymnbook in front of the building where you work. The idea that we might worship our work seems silly when we think of it in those terms.

Unfortunately, the idea of of worshiping work—that is, giving work dominion and sovereignty in our lives—isn't silly at all. Instead, it's frightening. It's frightening because we can so easily fall into its trap without knowing it.

What we're talking about is *treating work as an object of idolatry,* and the Bible is abundantly clear in its warnings against the worshiping of idols—any idols. Something becomes an idol in our lives when we give it the paramount importance and the reverence that should rightly be accorded only to God. When that concept or object assumes a place of sovereignty that God intended to be reserved for Himself alone, then we have replaced Him with an idol.

Does this sound extreme to you? Are you wondering how anyone could possibly fall into the trap of "worshiping" work?

Work meets different needs for different people. For some people it's the work itself that's satisfying. They like the challenge, the sense of self-worth and accomplishment, the teamwork, and the other intangible benefits of work. Maybe their work situation offers them prestige, authority, or power that they don't have in any other area of their lives.

For other people, work is simply an economic reality. Besides enabling them to meet their basic living expenses, work may also provide them with the money for the material possessions and the lifestyle they want. It enables them to give their children a Florida vacation or an expensive stereo. It provides possessions that enhance the enjoyment of leisure time: a boat or camping equipment or a motor home. It enables them to make their everyday lives more pleasant with a comfortable home and a good-looking, dependable car.

Work, and the rewards of our work, do a great deal more for us than simply enable us to eat and have roofs over our heads.

Is it wrong for us to enjoy our work itself, and/or to enjoy the material benefits that it makes possible? I don't think so. After all, God established work and gave it a role in our lives. Being "happy in our work" is a positive biblical concept. The value of work is scripturally identified.

So how, then, do we know whether work has its proper position in our lives, or whether it has assumed the role of an idol, dictating our spiritual goals instead of being shaped by them? I believe there are several criteria we can use to check up on our "work perspective."

1. Do work-related considerations drive the majority of our decisions?

As Christians, our decision-making should be rooted in the Scriptures and in our understanding of God's will, based on His Word and on our experience of Him. When we find ourselves making important decisions based more on how they will affect our work, or vice versa, than on a desire to do God's will, then work has encroached on God's place of sovereignty.

2. Are we requiring those around us to be governed by the demands of our work?

Wanda brings a lot of work home from her job as an accountant. She would like to be made a manager of the accounting office within a couple of years, so she feels it's important to show her dedication to the company by always going above and beyond in the amount of work she completes. Lately, though, it seems like every time her son or daughter asks if he or she can have a friend over, she finds herself saying, "No, you'll make too much noise, and I don't want to be disturbed while I'm working" or "I have too much work to do; I don't have time to pick your friends up and take them home."

Most of us have periods at work that are busier than others, and our families need to be flexible and help us cope with these busy times. We may need to work overtime or even take a second job to make ends meet. At those times we have little choice about how much of our time and energy is devoted to work. Often, though, we have more of a choice than we may think. To constantly allow our work responsibilities to dictate the whole family's activities and schedule, when in fact we have the choice to do otherwise, seems unfair to the other family members. When we routinely impose work-related restrictions on those around us without striving for a balanced lifestyle, we need to ask ourselves if perhaps we have let work assume a prominence in our family life that we don't really want it to have.

3. Is our total self-worth rooted in our work?

Remember Connie, the teacher who had to learn a hard lesson about the relationship of work and self-worth? I believe each of us has to relearn that lesson occasionally. Whether it's the work itself or its material rewards that make us feel good about ourselves, the fact remains that our inherent value comes from *God* and not from what we produce, achieve, or earn. Work has become an idol in our lives if we find ourselves relying on it for our sense of self-worth and importance.

4. *Are we sacrificing God's sacred trusts on the altar of work?*

God entrusts to us a great many things: the responsibility for raising children; the time, talent, and ability to respond to the needs of a desperate world; the opportunity to change individual lives, social conditions, and public policy; the talent to reveal Him to others in ways that only we can; the call to be His ambassadors to a world that doesn't know Him.

Work has become an idol when we are willing to sacrifice these trusts from God in the interests of pursuing our work and its rewards. One of the saddest scenarios in our society today is the picture of a child whose parents have worked hard to provide every material possession but sacrificed the one commodity their children want most: their presence. Equally sad is seeing the great number of people to whom God has given special talents and abilities, who use these only to advance their careers while the local church goes begging for individuals with the talents needed to carry out its programs in the community.

Work is a tool, a resource. It fills a great many needs in our lives, needs ranging from food and shelter to achievement and self-fulfillment. Like so many other tools that God gave us when He gave us dominion over the earth, work is something for us to use as we strive to respond to His call. We are to manage our work, not vice versa. When we let our work manage us instead, then we are in danger of falling into idolatry.

"Therefore speak to them and tell them, 'This is what the Sovereign LORD says: When any Israelite sets up idols in his heart and puts a wicked stumbling block before his face . . . I the LORD will answer him myself in keeping with his great idolatry' " (Ezekiel 14:4).

A Warning to the Up-and-Coming

"Highly motivated."

"A real self-starter."

"A go-getter."

"Always willing to go above and beyond to get the job done."

"Ambitious and hardworking."

If you were interviewing a person for a job opening at your company, wouldn't you be looking for some of these qualities?

Recently I met a young man who worked for one of the biggest entertainment companies in the world, and had a very responsible supervisory position. He had begun working for the company part-time while he was in college, and had been promoted nearly every year since then. For several of the promotions, he had not even applied but had simply been asked by the company if he would accept a new, higher position.

In talking with him, I could easily see why he had risen so rapidly through the corporate ranks. He came across as extremely personable, conscientious, loyal to the company, intelligent, and capable. A friend of mine used to say, "Some people are destined to reach the stars." This young man struck me as one of those.

I believe that the possibility of "reaching the stars" is a part of the American dream. A person who has "the right stuff" can rise through the ranks to the top, no matter how unpromising or how lowly his or her beginnings. In fact, I have personally known many individuals who have overcome tremendous obstacles—handicaps of background or birth or circumstance—and attained prominence, respect, and major accomplishments in their fields.

God gives us amazing capabilities, vast inner resources that enable us to do far more than even we ourselves imagine. I think it's exciting to contemplate the untapped possibilities that might lie within each of us, possibilities that we can bring to reality if we are willing to follow His commandments.

Some people, though, as they strive to succeed, to rise through the ranks, to accomplish or attain more and more, lose sight of the source of their abilities. They forget that it is only by God's love, mercy, and grace that we are able to achieve anything at all. Their destination becomes not fulfilling God's will for them, but meeting their own needs for recognition, power, prestige, wealth, influence, self-esteem, or the approval of others. The Bible calls this self-centered motivation "selfish ambition," and repeatedly warns against it. Because ambition is often viewed as a prerequisite of success, I think that understanding this concept of selfish ambition is important to our journey toward success.

The word "ambition" appears seven times in the New International Version of the Bible, but in only two of those times does it appear by itself. In all five of the remaining contexts it is accompanied by the word "selfish." I think that fact in itself holds a lesson for us.

In two of the verses, Romans 15:20 and 1 Thessalonians 4:11, the word "ambition" is used in the sense of a goal, a targeted accomplishment or behavior. Paul speaks of his ambition to forge new frontiers for the gospel. Later he suggests that living a quiet, industrious life is a worthy "ambition" for believers. The word is used in a neutral sense to refer to those goals.

In the remaining verses in which the word "ambition" occurs, it is preceded by "selfish." This suggests that ambition—like work, rest, and money—is neither good nor evil in itself. The *motive* which dictates that ambition determines its nature. A positive spiritual destination will produce positive ambitions; a wordly, self-serving destination will produce that kind of ambition.

The term "selfish ambition," however, suggests more than just a self-serving goal. "Selfish ambition" is an attitude, a mindset, a way of approaching not only work but life in general. It is an outlook that sees only one's own interests, goals, and desires and seeks to attain them regardless of the cost or consequence to others.

In Galatians 5:20, selfish ambition appears in a list of behaviors that Paul says result from man's sinful nature. It's not a pretty list; besides selfish ambition, it includes:

- Sexual immorality
- Impurity and debauchery
- Idolatry and witchcraft
- Hatred
- Discord
- Jealousy
- Fits of rage
- Dissensions and factions
- Envy
- Drunkenness, orgies, "and the like."

"I warn you, as I did before," Paul continues, "that those who live like this will not inherit the kingdom of God" (Galatians 5:21).

Selfish ambition keeps very unattractive company, doesn't it? The fact that it is grouped with a whole roster of sinful behavior should be a warning sign to us. Selfish ambition is shaped by sin and gives sin a route for obtaining a foothold in our lives. This sinful behavior then opens the door for others to follow, and gradually the "habit" of sin has become a large part of our lives.

Regina has her eye on her boss' job. Her boss, Elaine, is getting ready to retire, and Regina just knows that she could do a much better job in that position. Ever since she learned of Elaine's impending retirement, she's developed a one-track mind: She wants that job! Her salary would increase by over a third AND she would be promoted above the people she now works with. She loves to fantasize about the looks on their faces when they hear who's their new boss!

Regina is busily laying groundwork for her promotion, carrying out a carefully planned series of strategies during the six months before Elaine retires. She has her destination—Elaine's office—very clearly in mind, and she has set goals for meeting it.

Her first goal is to make sure she attracts positive notice from the vice-president who is Elaine's supervisor. So she has started sending him memos about tasks she has accomplished: increased cost savings in her area; a complimentary letter she received from a customer; going to an evening seminar to learn more about technology in her field. Elaine is bewildered by this sudden flow of memos over her head. She and Regina have always had a good relationship—or so she thought. She mentions the memos to Regina, who answers glibly, "Well, you're not going to be here forever, you know. I'm just acting on my motto, 'Be prepared.' " Elaine feels hurt and confused.

Another of Regina's goals is being sure the other vice-presidents hear lots of good ideas from her for improving the work of the unit—so that they'll react positively to her application for Elaine's job. When she sees them in the hallway, she'll always take the opportunity to say something like, "You know, I've been thinking about the problem we've been having with our mailing lists; I wondered if it would help if we sorted them by Zip code before we input the transaction codes." She doesn't mention that her "good ideas" are actually ones that she's picked up from her co-workers in casual conversation and then passed off as her own.

And so it goes. Just from these two examples of Regina's strategies, we can see that her selfish ambition has already led to hurting Elaine's feelings and "stealing" ideas from her co-workers (and then being dishonest about where they came from). Regina is so focused on herself that she just can't see what she's doing to others.

Suppose Regina's strategy works and she's promoted to Elaine's position. Will she have succeeded? Well, she will have accomplished her goals and reached her destination. I guess the world—maybe even including her coworkers—would call that success. But from a Christian perspective I don't think she will have been successful. Dishonesty and deceit and hurtfulness aren't components of the success to which God calls us.

I don't think Regina's desire to be promoted to Elaine's job was a *selfish* ambition in itself; it was just an ambition. Regina's motives, her strategies, and her whole perspective on the promotion made a neutral goal into a truly selfish ambition.

God calls us to do great things, and He gives us the ability to do them. When we seek His will and desire above all else to follow His plan and His commandments, then our ambition is pleasing to Him. But how can we avoid the pitfall of "selfish ambition" better than Regina did? I think we can avoid it if we remember three things.

1. Remember what God has done.

If Regina's play for Elaine's job is successful, we can almost see her congratulating herself on her cleverness and her "successful" plan. "I must be even smarter than I thought! I amaze myself sometimes!" she might say jokingly to herself. Believe it or not, God warned the Israelites about this same line of thought—that is, about the danger of beginning to think that their successes and achievements were the result of their own efforts or their own cleverness. He admonished them:

"Be careful that you do not forget the Lord your God, failing to observe his commands. . . . Otherwise, when you eat and are satisfied, when you build fine houses and settle down, and when your herds and flocks grow large and your silver and gold increase and all you have is multiplied, then your heart will become proud and you will forget the Lord your God, who brought you out of Egypt, out of the land of slavery" (Deuteronomy 8:11-14).

Do we remember to thank God for our accomplishments, our material possessions, our families, our freedom? Or have we begun to believe that we deserve or have earned these things, or that they are the result of our own doing?

2. *Remember where we are headed.*

Goals like Regina's can help keep us moving ahead and can challenge us to exercise our capabilities to the fullest. But if those goals become our destination instead of just milestones along the way, they can lead us into selfish ambition and idolatry. They can hide from our view the ultimate goal: serving and obeying God.

Any earthly attainments we might accrue during our lives are temporary, and the fulfillment and satisfaction that we might derive from them are temporary as well. This doesn't mean they aren't worthwhile; it only means that we can't rely on those achievements to see us through eternity. When we view them as part of our overall fulfillment of God's will for us, then they serve us in both this world and the next.

3. *Remember who we are.*

"I am a stranger on earth," the psalmist wrote (Psalm 119:19). God calls us to life that is different from the life the world would like us to live. Selfish ambition can seem acceptable to the world around us and can even earn us approval and rewards, as the Reginas of the world prove. The worship of work can impress others as diligence and company loyalty. The world tells us these qualities are good, but the Bible tells us they're not.

When God delivered the Israelites from Egypt and took them through other nations on their way to the promised land, He warned them not to adopt the customs, culture, and beliefs of those nations through which they passed. "You must not live according to the customs of the nations I am going to drive out before you. Because they did all these things, I abhorred them" (Leviticus 20:23). We too are traveling through an alien land—the world—on our way to eternity. The fact that we are here doesn't mean we have God's permission to live as those around us do. And that includes not letting ourselves be guided by the world's view of work, ambition, and success.

POINTS OF INTEREST

1. Besides a paycheck, what other positive values do you receive from your work? List these other benefits:

_____

_____

_____

_____

2. For each of the work-related values you listed above, think about another way you could receive the same things if your job were eliminated tomorrow.

_____

_____

_____

_____

3. How do you feel about the role of work in your life? Do you have the balance you would like to have, or do you think you need to make some changes? If so, what changes would you like to make?

_____

_____

_____

4. What specific steps could you take within the next 30 days to start bringing those changes about?

_____

_____

_____

5. How would you define "ambition" as it applies to you? Based on that definition, would you say you are—

(   ) Very ambitious

(   ) Fairly ambitious

(   ) Not particularly ambitious

(   ) Not ambitious at all

6. What do you think distinguishes positive ambition from selfish ambition?

_____

_____

7. Why do you think some people become workaholics? Have you ever felt that you were one or were becoming one? Why?

_____

_____

8. Could Regina have worked toward becoming a strong candidate for Elaine's job without succumbing to selfish ambition? List three strategies you would suggest to her (if she asked you) that would be in keeping with what God desires of us as women of God.

1. _____

2. _____

3. _____

9. Suppose you encouraged Regina to view being promoted as a milestone instead of a destination. Then what positive spiritual destination would you suggest to her that being promoted would help her reach?

_____

_____

10. What ways could you suggest to help each of us remember the three "things to remember" that we discussed at the end of this chapter?

_____

_____

SIGNPOST

Although they knew God,
they neither glorified him as God
nor gave thanks to him, but their
thinking became futile and their
foolish hearts were darkened. . . .
They exchanged the truth of God
for a lie, and worshiped and served
created things rather than the Creator—
who is forever praised.

—Romans 1:21, 25

I press on toward the goal
to win the prize for which God has called
me heavenward in Christ Jesus.

—Philippians 3:14

CHAPTER 7

God's Work Versus Paperwork

When we do the best we can,
we never know
what miracle is wrought in our life,
or in the life of another.

—Helen Keller

In Chapters 5 and 6 we talked a great deal about work and its role in our lives. There's one very important aspect of work we haven't explored yet, though, and we need to address it before we can proceed on our journey toward success. It's *the relationship of our work to God's work.* Understanding this relationship is essential to fully incorporating our work into our journey toward success.

What *is* God's work? Are there certain occupations that represent God's work more than others? With only 24 hours in a day, do we have time to do both His work and ours? Are they mutually exclusive, or can they be done at the same time? To succeed in God's sight, do I need to do His work rather than my earthly 9-to-5 job—or both? How do I know what work God would have me do for Him?

Let's start with a pop quiz about God's work versus our work.

The list below contains items describing tasks you might do in your workday. For each item, mark whether you think it belongs in the category of God's work (G) or the world's work (W).

(   ) Answering telephone calls
(   ) Assisting others with their work
(   ) Attending meetings
(   ) Dealing with customer complaints
(   ) Cleaning up the work area
(   ) Handling money
(   ) Inviting a new employee out to lunch
(   ) Leading a devotion or Bible study after work
(   ) Listening to a co-worker's problems
(   ) Meeting new people
(   ) Preparing documents (letters, reports, etc.)
(   ) Processing invoices
(   ) Responding to customers' complaints
(   ) Staying late to finish work
(   ) Telling a co-worker what God has done for you.

Now let's look at an assortment of occupations. Of the individuals listed below, which ones do you feel are doing God's work (G) and which ones are doing the world's work (W)? Write the appropriate letter by each occupation listed.

(   ) Actress
(   ) Accountant
(   ) Baker
(   ) Bank teller
(   ) Bookkeeper
(   ) Church secretary
(   ) Construction crew member
(   ) Invoice clerk
(   ) Minister

( ) Missionary
( ) Office manager
( ) Photographer
( ) Physician
( ) Nurse
( ) Public-relations executive
( ) Receptionist
( ) Sales manager
( ) Social worker
( ) Teacher
( ) Writer

Now let's make it harder. Within the occupations listed above, there could conceivably be some people who are doing God's work and some who aren't. How would you categorize the following individuals?

1. ( ) An award-winning actress whose movies are inspiring and uplifting, who devotes much of her time and considerable wealth to promoting more-liberal drug laws and pro-abortion legislation.

2. ( ) An award-winning actress whose R-rated movies contain explicit sex and bloody brutality, who organizes a national campaign to raise funds for the homeless.

3. ( ) A bookkeeper who handles the financial records for a community-supported shelter for abused women and children, although she could make a much higher salary in a private business.

4. ( ) A bookkeeper who works for a church but misrepresents how much the church receives in offerings and pockets the difference.

5. ( ) A minister for a large urban congregation, noted for his outstanding preaching and biblical scholarship, who makes sexual advances to women who come to him for counseling.

6. ( ) A physician who donates her services one day a week to the local free clinic for people who need health care but cannot pay for it.

7. ( ) A physician who encourages people to make numerous unnecessary return visits to her office and schedules his patients for tests they don't need, in order to increase his income.

8. ( ) A physician who does neither of the above, but simply cares for the medical needs of her patients to the best of her ability.

9. ( ) A receptionist in an insurance office who greets people courteously and helpfully, and tries to see that their business is handled promptly.

10. ( ) A receptionist in an insurance office who ignores people when they walk in the door and speaks to them rudely when they ask her a question.

Do you find that it's getting harder and harder to decide who's doing God's work and who isn't?

As you might have guessed, there's no set of correct answers to this quiz. The point is simply that God's work cannot be defined by our occupations or the kind of jobs we have. His work is more than that. But what *is* it? If one woman is a missionary and one is a dental hygienist, does that mean the former is doing God's work and the latter isn't? I don't think so.

In trying to understand what God's work is, it's interesting to trace the development of the biblical concept of work from the Old Testament through the New Testament. In the Old Testament, work enters the picture with Creation. God created the world and everything in it as "the work of his hands" (Psalm 19:1). That includes human beings.

Then, God began to talk to us about our own work, the work of *our* hands. Scripture suggests that when we obey God's commandments and seek to please Him, we will be "successful" in our work: 1) We will prosper— that is, we will benefit materially; 2) we will be able to complete the tasks we set out to do; and 3) we will reap the rewards of our labors. We will have what we need.

By contrast, however, if our work is motivated by evil

intentions or the work we do produces evil, we will not prosper or succeed. Instead, we will reap the consequences of disobeying God's statutes. "The Lord is known by his justice," the psalmist wrote; "the wicked are ensnared by the work of their hands" (Psalm 9:16).

Clearly we have to live with the consequences of the work that we do or don't do. The book of Proverbs emphasizes the importance of accepting work responsibilities and avoiding laziness: "One who is slack in his work is brother to one who destroys" (Proverbs 18:9).

When Jesus began His preaching ministry, though, He spoke of work—both God's and ours—in different terms. He introduced a new concept of work. No longer were God's work and man's work separate, but they merged into one work. Our earthly work is to do God's work.

"Do not work for food that spoils," Jesus taught, "but for food that endures to eternal life, which the Son of Man will give you."

When the people asked Him, "What must we do to do the works God requires?" Jesus replied, "The work of God is this: to believe in the one he has sent" (John 6:27-29).

Doesn't that make the whole issue much simpler? This is one of my favorite verses in all of Scripture regarding the role of work in our lives. The tasks we complete each day don't determine whether we are doing God's work. The prestige of our job title or position isn't the deciding factor. Whether we spend our days answering phones, filing papers, doing open-heart surgery, making million-dollar financial decisions, or teaching a classroom full of preschoolers doesn't make any difference in whether or not we are doing God's work. It's the *vision*, the *ultimate desired result that we bring to those tasks* that consecrates them to God.

For those of us who are mothers, the same is true for

our parenting role. The circumstance of being a mother isn't doing God's work; it's a biological occurrence. We do God's work as mothers when we teach our children to obey His teachings and to honor Christ's sovereignty in their lives.

What makes the difference? What distinguishes work that is simply an earthly task from God's work? Jesus said that God's work is "to believe in the One He has sent." But how does that translate into our day-to-day lives?

How's the View from There?

When we perform our earthly work in a context of faith, the way we view that work is affected. Our work is a gift both *to* God and *from* God, since He is the One who gives us the resources to do it. The physical capacity to perform tasks, the intellectual ability to learn skills, the hours in the day to do our jobs—in fact, our very lives— all come from God and are entrusted to us as resources from Him. The earthly work we do is a testimony to Him, a return on what He has entrusted to us. Can we afford to let it be any less than our very best?

Whether we view our work as just a means to an end— financial, professional, or personal—or whether it's important to our sense of well-being and challenge, it consumes a great deal of our time, energy, and ability. In terms of clock-hours alone, it's too big a component of our lives for us to set it apart from God, to compartmentalize it in a way that says "hands off" to Him. When we instead view our work as a sacrifice to God, a gift at His altar, then our desire is to make that sacrifice as perfect and unblemished as we can, and to insure that it is the product of our very best effort.

"Whatever you do, work at it with all your heart, as working for the Lord, not for men, since you know that you will receive an inheritance from the Lord as a reward" (Colossians 3:23,24).

I'm Doing the Best I Can!

Does a Christian whose work is consecrated to God act any different in the workplace from everyone else? Is her work product any different? Maybe and maybe not. Certainly there are others around us at work who are highly motivated to do a good job. Perhaps they're simply conscientious by nature. Maybe they're hoping for a promotion or a raise. Maybe they have a competitive urge that pushes them to do better than someone else. You don't have to be a Christian to perform well on the job.

Yet a Christian in the workplace *should* be different.

Jesus said that we are not "of the world." If we are the same as those who don't know Christ, how can we fulfill our role as His ambassadors, His representatives to unbelievers around us in the workplace? "We are therefore Christ's ambassadors, as though God were making his appeal through us" (2 Corinthians 5:20).

Ruthie is proofreading the accounting department's quarterly report before her boss turns it in to the company president. The report says the department collected 1300 dollars in overdue payments from customers. She knows the department head has been under a great deal of pressure from the president to reduce the overdue accounts, and the whole department has been working extra-hard on collections. That 1300-dollar figure sounds way too low; she wonders if it's a typing error and the actual figure is 13 *thousand* dollars. Based on what she's seen and heard during the quarter, that seems like a more likely total.

The report is due tomorrow, but the woman who typed it has left for the day. The backup material for the report has been filed, but all Ruthie would need to do would be to re-add the figures and check the total.

But it's 4:00 in the afternoon. The figures in the report really aren't her responsibility, after all. The department head is the one who should be checking to insure that the figures are right. If the error comes to light later, she can just say she thought it had already been checked and that she shouldn't change it.

If you were Ruthie, what would you do? Does it make a difference to view your work as a sacrifice that you present each day to God? What would it take for you to feel good about offering your work on the report to Him as your gift?

God doesn't expect perfection; He knows we aren't capable of it. People who are perfectionists in their day-to-day work often create unnecessary stress for themselves through their unrealistic expectations (and I should know—ask the people I work with).

I do believe, though, that when it comes to our earthly work, we have the opportunity to be witnesses for Him, showing the world what it means to live a life consecrated to God. If we don't care about the quality of our work, which we are being paid to do, how can we convince others that we care about the quality of our spiritual lives, or the quality of theirs, or the quality of where we'll spend eternity? If we don't demonstrate patience under pressure, or love in the face of conflict, or self-control under provocation, how can we reveal the fruit of a Christ-centered life? The Bible doesn't suggest that we pick and choose the areas of our lives in which to please God. I don't believe that we can just "get by" in our earthly jobs and tell ourselves that our attitudes and our actions don't matter to Him. Those hours we spend at work are precious; God has entrusted them to us and has given us the resources to use them. At the end of the day, I don't want to be ashamed to lay before Him what I have done with His trust.

There's a World Out There

Apart from our 9-to-5 jobs, there's another facet to doing God's work. If, as Jesus said, the work of God is believing in Christ, then it follows that we must also obey Christ's mandate to care for others. While Scripture clearly teaches that we do not have to work to earn God's approval, it also teaches that He expects us to be His hands and feet in meeting the needs of others.

In our hectic lives—our constant juggling act of home, family, job, and personal demands—we must find time to do the "good works" to which God calls us. This may mean volunteering at a hospital or helping raise funds for a children's home. It may mean working in the church nursery or teaching Sunday school. Good works don't have to be formalized and structured, though. Making a casserole for a convalescing neighbor or holding someone's hand when a loved one has died are also part of carrying out His commandment of love and caring.

God calls us to "look after orphans and widows in their distress" (James 1:27). Jesus made it clear that part of our mission as His followers is to feed the hungry, give water to the thirsty, shelter the stranger, clothe the naked, and visit the sick and imprisoned. These are the acts of a person committed to God's commandment of love and compassion—believing "in the One he has sent." But these are not prerequisites to salvation. God's grace is a free gift, not a reward for good deeds. We do not have to do "good works" in order to earn His love; we do them *because* of His love.

How does all this help us define success?

I believe that we cannot fully carry out God's will and be successful in His sight without doing His work. Yet we frustrate ourselves and get our own lives off course when we become confused about what His work is. His work is *not* defined as being a perfect individual. Neither is His work defined as being a minister or a missionary, although certainly He needs people willing to pursue those callings. His work *is whatever we do in belief, love, and faith, consecrating it to Him as a return on His trust to us.* We can do His work at home—as spouses, parents, single women, married women, young women, or old women.

We can do His work in our places of employment, whether we assemble complex machinery or counsel drug abusers. We can do His work in our churches, in our neighborhoods, and in our political system.

We can even do His work if we are ill or disabled and can only lie in a hospital bed, praying for the world around us or simply demonstrating faith and courage in dealing with pain and physical limitations.

Being a successful woman of God begins with belief . . . and continues through eternity. It is indeed a journey, not a destination. We do His work along the way, succeeding in drawing closer to Him and representing Him to the world. As we do so, we gain a better grasp of what it means to be servants—servants of God and of mankind. After all, Jesus told us that success begins with servanthood.

POINTS OF INTEREST

1. In this chapter we discussed the fact that Christians aren't the only ones motivated to do good work on the job. What other forces might motivate a person to perform her job well?

_____

_____

_____

_____

2. As long as the result is the same, does it matter whether we are motivated by a desire to please God or by some other movitation?

_____

_____

_____

3. Make yourself a note to reflect, at the end of your next workday, on how you spent your time that day and the work you did. Is it an offering that you can gladly lay on God's altar, or is there something you'd like to change about it if you could? What could you do to bring that change about for tomorrow's workday?

_____

_____

_____

4. Are you a perfectionist? What problems does being a perfectionist cause on the job? How can a perfectionist learn to be more realistic about her standards, but at the same time still put forth her best effort in her work? If it's

not perfection that God wants, what approach does He want us to take in our work?

_____

_____

_____

5. For you, what does doing God's work entail?

_____

_____

_____

6. It's been several chapters since we reevaluated our earlier definitions of success. Go back now to Chapter 1 and review the definition you wrote. If you feel that it needs changing, write a revised definition here:

_____

_____

_____

SIGNPOST

*When the kindness and love of God
our Savior appeared, he saved us,
not because of righteous things we had done,
but because of his mercy.*

—Titus 3:4,5

*We continually remember before our God
and Father your work produced by faith,
your labor prompted by love,
and your endurance inspired by hope
in our Lord Jesus Christ.*

—1 Thessalonians 1:3

PART THREE

Some Rules of the Road

CHAPTER 8

Learning to Think Upside Down

*After the verb "to love,"
"to help" is the most beautiful verb
in the world.*

—Bertha von Suttner

(If you don't have a pencil handy, you might want to get one before you begin this chapter. You'll need it for the short exercise that follows.)

In the spaces on the next page, make two lists. In the first list write the names of the five most *successful* people you can think of. Don't spend a lot of time weighing one against another or trying to come up with "good" answers; just jot down the first five that come to mind. Ready? Go!

In the second column write the names of the five people you *admire most*. They can be well-known people or unknowns, people you know personally or people you've never met.

List 1   **List 2**

_____   _____

_____   _____

What do you think—should these two lists be the same? After all, if people are successful, we admire them, don't we? Isn't success an achievement worthy of admiration? And if we admire people, then they must be successful at *something*, right?

Compare your two lists. How many names appear on both lists? One? Two? All five?

Think about the people you listed as those you admire. What is it that you admire about them? When I think of "admiration," I think of wanting to be in some way like that person I admire. He or she has qualities I wish I had, or that I wish I possessed to a greater degree. For example, I don't automatically admire people who accumulate great wealth, but if their wealth is a by-product of exceptional creativity and integrity and self-discipline, then I might admire them for those qualities.

Who's in the Top Ten?

Of the many public opinion polls taken in our country each year, one that especially interests me is the "Ten Most Admired" poll. In this poll, Americans are asked to name the ten men and the ten women they admire most.

While business figures like Lee Iacocca appear in this listing from time to time, there are four individuals who over the years have invariably appeared near the top of the list: evangelist Billy Graham, Mother Teresa of Calcutta, and the President and First Lady of the United States, whoever they might be at the time.

I always feel encouraged when I see the results of this poll, because I feel reassured that Americans still admire something besides the accumulation of material wealth. Isn't it ironic that in a culture as preoccupied with success as ours is, the people we most admire are *servants*? Billy Graham is, first and foremost, a servant of the gospel. Mother Teresa is unquestionably a servant of mankind and of God. And the President and First Lady of the United States, whatever their political stance, are above all else servants of the American people.

Movie stars and other entertainers show up in the "Most Admired" polls from time to time too, but only those stars who have used their fame and financial resources in support of "causes"—alleviating world hunger, saving the environment, promoting peace. In their own way, these individuals of fame and wealth have chosen to be servants also.

I like the idea that the people in this country admire those who devote their lives to service. I feel encouraged to know that, deep down, we as a nation believe there is value in servanthood—because according to Jesus, that's the first prerequisite to success.

How Can You Get to the Top by Staying at the Bottom?

When we talk about success, we always talk in terms of "reaching the top." We describe people's progress toward success as a climb up the corporate ladder or a rise to the top of their field of work. If you look at the organizational chart of any business, the position at the top of the chart is the one with the most power, the one that represents success for the person who attains it.

Another common expression in talking about success is that "the cream rises to the top"; that is, the richest, best part of a bucket of milk is found at the top. Since the way we talk about things often shapes our thinking about them, we naturally think of success as being at the top.

And then along comes Jesus and disrupts everything. Oh, He has a formula for success, all right, but it wasn't at all what His listeners back in the year 28 or 29 A.D. wanted to hear, and it doesn't conform to popular thinking about success today, either.

Being human, Jesus' disciples were a little on the competitive side, particularly the "Sons of Thunder," James and John. They weren't what you would call laid-back guys. They were *doers*—energetic, aggressive, action-oriented. They didn't like doing things halfway. If they were going to participate in this kingdom that Jesus promised, they wanted to do it in a big way, so they asked Jesus to give them positions of high authority in His kingdom. They figured that would be major success: having a position right next to the ruler of a heavenly kingdom.

But Jesus didn't grant their request. Instead, He introduced a whole new concept of success, one that literally turned conventional thinking upside down.

"You know that those who are regarded as rulers of the Gentiles lord it over them, and their high officials exercise authority over them. Not so with you. Instead, whoever wants to be great among you must be your servant, and whoever wants to be first must be slave of all. For even the Son of Man did not come to be served, but to serve, and to give his life as a ransom for many" (Mark 10:42-45).

Wait a minute. To be great—to be successful—I have to be a *servant*? A *slave*?

Just think how topsy-turvy this must have appeared to the people of Jesus' time, a time when servants were viewed more as possessions than people and had none of what we today consider basic human rights. Their only function was to serve their masters' every whim. Slaves weren't at the bottom rung of society's ladder; they weren't on the ladder at all! And Jesus says that if we want to be at the top, we have to be like them: lower than the bottom. We have to learn to serve.

A Look Inside the Heart of a Servant

Years ago, when I was teaching journalism, there was a young woman named Dawn in one of my classes. She was a talented writer, an insightful thinker, a capable and disciplined student. I knew she would make it as a journalist in the business world. She was destined for success.

But Dawn had another kind of success in mind. When she graduated from college, she became a missionary with an international evangelistic organization. Fluent in Spanish, she took special training to present the gospel to Spanish-speaking communities in North, Central, and South America. Eventually she married a journalist who was a missionary with the same organization, and together they continued their ministry. Now, with a baby daughter, they have just accepted a new assignment in Latin America.

The last time I talked to Dawn, which was about a year ago, I tried to tell her how proud I am of her, how awed I have been as I have watched the course of her life. I tried to describe what a source of inspiration she is to me. "I'm proud just to know you," I told her.

Afterward I thought about what specific quality in Dawn was most inspiring, and the answer was clear: Dawn truly has the heart of a servant. Her life is a shining example of what it means to serve God and to serve others. Her work, her goals, and her destination all reflect that desire to serve.

Dawn's periodic, newsy letters that she sends to her friends and financial supporters constantly give me new insights into the nature of servanthood. She writes of the difficult decisions that she and her husband face about where to go next, what new mission field God would have them enter. She tells of their material needs being miraculously met by God's grace—car expenses, finding a place to live, raising enough money to finance their move to a new location. She even wrote of the terror of being separated from her husband and imprisoned in a Central American jail after being deceived by a corrupt government official.

Dawn's faithfulness to God, her willingness to put the needs of others before her own desires, and her total commitment to doing God's work continue to inspire me. Through her I have had a glimpse of what Jesus meant when He called us to be servants.

But I Thought God Wanted Us to Be Free!

Fortunately, our country long ago abolished the practice that allowed people to own other human beings. God created men and women in His image, with dignity and worth, and this knowledge made slavery intolerable.

The spiritual servanthood that Christ talked about isn't just another form of earthly slavery. Unfortunately, though, confusion about the meaning of servanthood persists, and people continue to view it in a negative light because they equate it with the historical concept of slavery.

In addition, since the earliest days of the women's movement, feminists have given a negative tone to the whole concept of serving others, especially in the home and in the workplace. Feminist literature has portrayed women as slaves of men, shackled by traditions in a male-dominated world. Women are depicted as toiling from dawn to dusk without reward or recognition, while men receive all the benefits of their labors.

The women's movement has exhorted us to throw off

this enslavement and seize our place of equality in the world. Cooking, doing laundry, caring for children, and other domestic tasks have been labeled drudgery that stifles women's potential; we have been pressured to give them up in favor of other roles outside the home that will enable us to "fulfill" ourselves. In doing so, women have taken on a whole new set of problems and frustrations as we have pursued the rewards that have traditionally been reserved for men. And somewhere along the line, as far as women are concerned, the concept of servanthood has gone out of vogue.

I believe wholeheartedly—in fact, I know—that there are women who have been victims of injustice in the workplace, just as there are men who have been victims of injustice. I know, too, that there are husbands who make unreasonable demands on their wives, just as there are wives who make unreasonable demands on their husbands. I believe that people who do the same work with the same ability should be paid the same for it, and that all people should be free to make choices about their lives to whatever extent that is possible; after all, free will is part of God's design for us. And I'm the first to agree that frying bacon and sorting muddy socks can be, well, less than exciting.

However, I also believe that if women *or* men convince themselves that a spirit of servanthood has no place in our society and no place in our individual lives, then we will all be the losers. If we view all household tasks as drudgery, instead of as ways of serving those we love, then drudgery is what they'll be. If we view being of service to our employers as an infringement on our independence, then our hours on the job will be dismal indeed.

Worse yet, if we flatly reject the notion of servanthood because we can't separate it from slavery, we still won't be free at all; we will only be enslaved by a different philosophy, a selfish and bitterly lonely philosophy that urges us to view life as one long, defensive battle to protect our own rights.

*See to it that no one takes you captive
through hollow and deceptive philosophy,
which depends on human tradition
and the basic principles of this world
rather than on Christ.*

—Colossians 2:8

As Christians, women or men, we cannot escape the call to servanthood. God's first commandment to us is to serve Him. Jesus' greatest commandments to us are to love and serve God and to love and serve others. This twofold servanthood is fundamental to the Christian life.

Not all of us are called to serve God and others in exactly the way Dawn is, but each of us *is* called to serve. The Bible illustrates for us the qualities that should characterize our lives as we fulfill God's first commandment: to serve Him.

1. Commitment to the Master's interests.

The parable of the talents in Matthew 25 reveals that the good servant was the one who looked out for his master's interests, even when his master wasn't there to watch over him. That servant had made his master's interests his own; what was important to his master was important to him. Are God's interests important to us?

2. Willingness to work.

The servant in Matthew 25 didn't just sit around while his master was away; he took action to advance his master's interests. Giving lip service or even mental and philosophical assent to God's commandments isn't enough; a good servant must be willing to act for the good of his master. As the biblical writer James says, "Do not merely listen to the word, and so deceive yourselves. Do what it says" (1:22).

3. Obedience.

A good servant does what she is told to do, so that the master's ends can be achieved. She doesn't argue about the merit of the request or weigh whether she feels like doing it just then; she does it, obediently. Doing God's work isn't a matter of convenience or expedience, but of obedience.

4. Loyalty.

An ideal servant is loyal, not being persuaded or bribed to do something to harm or cheat his master. That servant can be counted on if the master is in need or in trouble; he would actively seek what was best for his master and his master's household.

Every day we are surrounded by temptations to compromise God's commandments, to let the world "bribe" us to cheat God. If we are to be effective servants, we must be faithful ones.

5. A spirit of sacrifice.

A faithful servant would be willing to sacrifice her own desires, if necessary, to insure the master's well-being. A servant's loyalty might even extend to risking or sacrificing her life for her master. All that we have comes from God; anything we give up or lose for His sake we are simply giving back to Him.

When it comes to the second great commandment—to love and serve others—we have to remind ourselves once again that spiritual servanthood is not the same as enslavement of one human being by another. Because we are human and our understanding is limited, this is hard for us to grasp; we try to equate God's principles with earthly experiences and thereby misinterpret them. However, unless we are able to make a clear distinction between spiritual servanthood and earthly slavery, we won't be able to understand the concept of serving in the sense that God intends for us. Let's look at the differences:

First, *spiritual servanthood is the result of a choice.*

God gives us choices. One of the keys to spiritual maturity is learning to choose what is right in God's eyes. Choosing to serve or not to serve is one of those choices. If, however, we choose to serve God, then we are called to serve other people as well.

By contrast, slavery is not a choice. It is a life condition forced on a person by someone else of superior power or strength. God does not force Himself on us. Our choice of spiritual servanthood is part of our response to His love and His call in our lives.

SIGNPOST

*Choose for yourselves this day
whom you will serve . . . .
But as for me and my household,
we will serve the LORD."*

—Joshua 24:15

Second, *spiritual servanthood is rooted in the conviction that we are important to God.*

Earthly slavery denies the fundamental value of human beings. Spiritual servanthood, by contrast, stems from the unique relationship that we have with God as His children.

God created human beings differently from animals. Unlike them, we are made in God's image. He made us "a little lower than the angels," and entrusted the whole earth to us (not that we have been very responsible stewards!). He ultimately showed His love for us by sacrificing His Son so that we might be free to experience the life He wants for us. He continues to demonstrate His love on a daily basis through His Spirit, His forgiveness, and His grace. Does this sound like an earthly master-slave relationship?

It's true that God is our Master in the sense that He holds absolute, unfathomable power over us. But He exercises that power in love, for our well-being, and always leaves us the freedom to make choices about how and to what extent we will serve Him. One of the countless mysteries of faith is this: The more we acknowledge His sovereignty in our lives by practicing servanthood, the freer we become.

Third, *spiritual servanthood has its own rewards.*

A slave received nothing for his labors. Even his food and shelter might be withheld when his master was displeased. Similarly, spiritual servanthood is not something we adopt in the hope of being rewarded. Yet the great irony is that when we truly serve, expecting nothing in return, rewards flow out from God's abundance. These rewards include:

- *Spiritual growth.* Like other aspects of Christian living, the practice of servanthood leads to spiritual maturity, to greater insight, and above all to a closer walk with God.
- *Positive relationships with other people.* The qualities that are part of being a Christian servant—among

them compassion, generosity, kindness, love, and fairness—are the qualities on which good relationships are built. By contrast, the opposite qualities—self-centeredness, unkindness, jealousy, prejudice, vindictiveness—only build a foundation for conflict, tension and pain.

- *Testimony to those around us.* The apostle Paul called us "ambassadors for Christ." When we fail to follow the world's rules of me-firstism and success-at-any-price, and instead demonstrate a spirit of serving, others begin to notice that our lives are different from those of other people, giving them a glimpse of Christ through us.

A Servant's Place Is . . . Everywhere

Since Brenda and Tom both have full-time jobs outside the home, they've worked out an arrangement in which they take turns being responsible for fixing dinner for a week at a time. This week it's Tom's turn. It's 6 P.M. on Thursday night and he's not home yet; usually he's home by 5:30. Brenda has come home and changed into a pair of jeans, and is relaxing with a book, enjoying the peace and quiet after a busy workday. She's tired, and she's glad it's Tom's night to cook.

About ten minutes past six Tom calls to say he'll be home in a few minutes; he's spent the last half-hour with a disgruntled customer who walked in the door at 5:30 P.M. and ranted and raved for a half-hour about how he was overcharged on his last bill (which he wasn't). Tom's voice is filled with frustration and fatigue.

If you were Brenda, what would you do?

- a) Stick with the plan. It's Tom's night to cook, after all. You're just as tired as he is, and you'll be cooking all next week.
- b) Fix dinner and have Tom cook *next* Thursday in return.

c) Just fix dinner.

d) Start getting things ready for dinner so Tom can just finish up when he gets home.

e) Wait until Tom comes home and suggest that the two of you go out for hamburgers (if it's in the budget).

Spiritual servanthood isn't just something for us to ponder and meditate on; it's a way of *thinking and acting in our day-to-day lives*. It doesn't have to mean:

- Waiting hand and foot on our husbands and then resenting their lack of cooperation around the house.
- Doing everything for our children, so that they never learn to be self-sufficient and independent.
- Staying up all night folding socks and underwear, knowing that we have an early meeting at work in the morning.
- Forgoing that fitness class or Bible study because "there's too much to do at home."
- Taking on someone else's work at the office because she's isn't willing to put forth the effort to get it done.

Spiritual servanthood does mean a willingness to serve others out of genuine sensitivity and concern for their needs *and* an awareness of what God expects of us. Let's evaluate each of Brenda's options listed above:

a) Rigid adherence to the every-other-week plan puts Brenda's "rights" ahead of Tom's needs. It makes the rules more important than the people. The apostle Paul repeatedly emphasized that God wants us to be free from this kind of legalistic thinking. "But now . . . we have been released from the law so that we serve in the new way of the Spirit, and not in the old way of the written code" (Romans 7:6).

b) To help Tom out by fixing dinner, and then requiring him to repay the favor, isn't servanthood but scorekeeping.

c), d), and e) I think any of these are good options.

Brenda's actual choice would depend on the couple's finances, the amount of work involved in fixing dinner, how tired she is herself, and other considerations.

Think about some situations in your own life where an attitude of servanthood would make a difference in how you respond. What relationships at home, or at work, or elsewhere would benefit from a spirit of serving on your part?

As we try to better understand the impact of servanthood on our everyday lives, let's talk about some things that biblical servanthood *isn't*. I believe that our failure to understand what servanthood *isn't* is largely to blame for the negative connotations it has accumulated through the women's movement and other self-fulfillment philosophies.

1. Servanthood is not blind obedience to earthly authority.

Suppose your boss walks into the office tomorrow and says, "I've figured out a way to embezzle 500,000 dollars from this company, and I need you to help me. Here's what you need to do." Then he proceeds to explain your role in his scheme. Does your Christian commitment to servanthood mean that you just say "You're the boss!" and proceed? Of course not.

One of God's gifts to us is the power of insight and discernment. Certainly part of being a servant in the practical day-to-day sense means being a willing and conscientious worker on the job, since the Bible clearly states that we are to obey earthly authorities—which includes employers, bosses, and supervisors. However, the Bible also makes it clear that when those authorities require actions that conflict with God's commands, "we must obey God rather than men" (Acts 5:29).

2. Servanthood is not a total disregard for your own needs.

If your child asks you for something to drink, do you give him an empty glass? No—because that won't meet his need.

Similarly, if we are to help meet the needs of God's kingdom and of those around us, we cannot let ourselves become empty. Unlike God, human beings have physical and emotional needs. We cannot function indefinitely without food or water or rest. Nor can we live consistently useful, satisfying lives if we neglect our own emotional and spiritual needs.

Women often run the risk of this neglect because of the nurturing, caregiving role that we so often fulfill, not just within our families but often at work and elsewhere as well. Yet we cannot maintain our capacity to care for others—to serve others—if we do not also care for ourselves.

Continually choosing to meet others' needs *at the expense of our own* is neither a healthy nor a spiritually sound way to live. Taking the time for an exercise class that improves your health and mental outlook isn't being selfish, it's being sensible. Asking someone to stay with your children occasionally while you attend a Bible study or go shopping with a friend isn't being a neglectful parent, it's treating yourself like a human being. Telling your daughter you can't make cookies for the Christmas party when you have a miserable cold isn't being irresponsible; it's accepting reality. We must learn to care for ourselves with sensitivity and compassion if we are to serve others. Finding and maintaining balance between the two is a lifelong challenge.

3. Servanthood is not passive hostility.

"I'll do it, but I won't like it" is the theme song of the passively hostile person. She acquiesces to what is asked of her—by her employer, her spouse, her children, her community, her church, her club—but she simmers and fumes with resentment the whole time. She can be unpleasant to be around and difficult to work with. When she does you a favor, she makes her resentment so obvious that you'd much rather do it yourself.

Some people treat God this way. They resent what they view as His "demands" on them. They grumble about going to church and especially resent it if they're asked to serve the church in some way. They feel oppressed if their conscience prompts them to do a kind deed for someone else.

Fran is an example. "I suppose I should take some soup over to Mr. Henry next door, since he's been sick," she'll say, then add, "I don't know how I'm going to find the time—and he's such a talker. I'll never get out of there." She's easily offended by others who unwittingly remind her of what God expects of her.

"That Joyce—she's always acting so pious and goody-goody," Fran complains. "I was telling her the latest gossip at work about Brenda getting fired, and all she said was, 'I'll bet Brenda felt pretty bad. Maybe I'll give her a call.' Joyce's attitude is so irritating."

4. *Servanthood is not a suffering-martyr syndrome.*

Joanne is the office martyr. Whenever the office work load gets extra heavy, she heaves a sigh and says she'll stay late and do it. The next morning she'll tell you how tired she is because she had to work so late.

When all the women in the department are going out to lunch for someone's birthday, Joanne volunteers to stay behind and answer the phone. Then, when the group comes back, she'll ask them all about the luncheon and say sadly, "I sure wish I had been there."

Joanne's "martyrdom" stems not from God's call to servanthood but from her own decision. Perhaps she believes that this "serving" behavior will make people like her better, or maybe it gives her a way to reassure herself that she's a nice person. Whatever the reason, it appears that Joanne's servanthood has less to do with God's expectations than with her own need to be liked and to feel good about herself.

While Joanne's co-workers appreciate her helpfulness, her attitude of martyrdom has alienated them. When they offer to do things to help *her*, of course, she won't hear of it. As a result they've begun to feel that they're continually indebted to her, and no one likes to be put in that position. They really wish she would back off a little.

Joanne, like many of us, seems to be doing the right thing, but for the wrong reason. If she could stop working so hard to win other people's approval, and focus on simply being the person God wants her to be, she could free herself from her martyr role and begin to learn more about real servanthood.

5. Servanthood is not a way to manipulate other people.

Have you ever been in a meeting or some other group setting and seen a "yes-woman" at work? She's the one who always emphatically agrees with whoever is the most influential in the group or whoever's viewpoint will benefit her personally the most. She'll be the first to volunteer for a high-visibility, low-workload position in the women's club. She'll take on an additional project the boss wants done, and then be sure everyone knows what a hard worker she is. She can be counted on to help you out when you're trying to finish a big report—but then she'll take credit for a lot more of it than she actually produced. She'll do you a favor when you're in a jam, but then she'll be sure to remind you of it when she needs something from you.

This kind of person has the appearance of being willing to serve others, but is actually self-serving. Her motive isn't genuine concern for the needs of those around her or the interests of her employer or her club; she's motivated by her desire to meet her own objectives by manipulating other people.

Unfortunately, this kind of false servanthood is sometimes rewarded in the workplace because it gives the appearance of loyalty and dedication to the employer. But as my friend Ava says, "What goes around comes around." People will not be fooled by this pretense for very long, and of course God will not be fooled at all.

The servanthood to which Christ calls us is none of these things. Instead, it is giving without any expectation of return. It is loving without any assurance of being loved back. It is performing a kindness simply because the kindness was needed. It is a quality that we by ourselves do not possess, but one that Christ teaches us and the Holy Spirit creates in us.

We discover a capacity for true servanthood only when we let God empower us to serve Him and others. Then there is no limit to what we can do. Servanthood is indeed the foundation of real success. Servanthood means keeping our eye on the destination: following God's commandments and doing His will. When we focus on serving Him and serving others, in the process we become less entangled in the petty frustrations and setbacks of day-to-day life. We have a sense of perspective that helps keep us on course in our journey toward success.

An Angel with a Bucket

This past weekend I learned yet another lesson about the nature of servanthood, and received a reminder that sometimes God teaches us things under very strange circumstances.

My son, Matthew, had had a friend stay overnight Saturday night, and the next morning we all left for the early church service. We were a little late, and the service had already begun when we reached the church, so there was no one around. When we got out of the car across the street from the church, my son's friend said, "I don't feel very well. My stomach hurts."

"When we get inside," I said, "you can sit down and maybe you'll feel better."

Well, he didn't make it inside. He threw up on the church steps.

Now, if you are a mother, this won't surprise you. In fact, you probably have a similar story from the annals of your own family's history. But this story took an interesting turn.

There I was, standing outside the church, turning green and trying to decide what to do. I told my son to stay with his friend, and I went inside to find the church custodian. Luckily, I happened to catch him in the hallway. I told him what had happened, and he went to get some cleaning supplies.

When I went back outside, though, I was astonished to see that the mess was gone, and Matthew's friend was sitting on a bench drinking a glass of orange soda.

"Where did you get the soda?" I asked him.

"That man gave it to me," he answered, "and he cleaned up the steps."

He was pointing at a dark-haired man with a broad smile who was coming across the street carrying a pail of water.

"I see what happen from my apartment right across the street," he said with a heavy accent. "I clean it up and bring him a drink." He walked over to the steps and threw the water down to wash away the remaining debris.

"Thank you," I said, handing him the now-empty soda glass. "You are so kind. Thank you so much."

Still smiling cheerfully, he turned and headed back to his apartment. "Jesus paid," he said to me over his shoulder. "Jesus paid for all of us."

I had just seen a true servant at work.

POINTS OF INTEREST

1. Can you think of someone you know personally who you feel exemplifies the spirit of servanthood? Jot down two examples of things which this person has done that show a willingness to serve God and/or other people.

_____

_____

_____

_____

_____

2. Why do you think the idea of being a "servant" is hard for people to accept? Is it hard for you to accept? Why?

_____

_____

_____

_____

3. Think of something specific you could do this week to put the spirit of servanthood into practice—at home, at work, or in a certain relationship or situation. Note it below and make a commitment to doing it. Afterward, think about how it made you feel. What were the results or consequences?

_____

_____

_____

_____

4. Jesus led the life of a servant of God and of mankind. What examples of servanthood from His life come to mind?

_____

_____

_____

_____

_____

5. Is there any area of your life in which you might be practicing false or self-serving servanthood? If so, examine your motives and ask God to teach you more about real servanthood. Be ready to accept His forgiveness and His help as you seek to change and grow spiritually.

Prayer: Lord, teach me to have the heart of a servant. Give me a willingness to serve others, and above all to serve You in sincerity and love. Amen.

6. Go back to the definitions of success you wrote at the end of Chapter 1 and Chapter 7. How does servanthood figure into that definition? If you want to rewrite the definition to reflect something you've learned in this chapter about servanthood, do it now:

_____

_____

_____

_____

_____

_____

_____

SIGNPOST

*You, my brothers, were called
to be free. But do not use your freedom
to indulge the sinful nature;
rather, serve one another
in love.*

—Galatians 5:13

*Your attitude should be the same
as that of Christ Jesus:
Who, being in very nature God,
did not consider equality
with God something to be grasped,
but made himself nothing,
taking the very nature of a servant,
being made in human likeness.*

—Philippians 2:5-7

CHAPTER 9

When Enough Is Enough— And When It Isn't

I never notice what has been done. I only see what remains to be done.

—Marie Curie

Y ou're just leaving aerobics class after a grueling workout. Your legs feel like they each weigh about the same as a steel beam. You wonder if it's possible for a person to perspire to death, and hope it isn't.

"I thought that class would never end," you moan. "I've definitely had enough."

"Not me," chirps your classmate Terry. "I'm going to go play racquetball now."

*   *   *

It's your brother's birthday, and your mother has invited the whole family over for a birthday dinner. She's fixed chicken and dumplings, green beans, corn casserole, homemade rolls, and baked sweet potatoes. You lean back from the table feeling like a new sofa pillow.

"That was great, Mom," you say. "I think I've eaten enough to last me a week."

"Nonsense," she says. "We still have cake and ice cream to go."

*   *   *

The president of the small manufacturing company you work for announces at an employee meeting that the company has had an exceptionally good year. He then proceeds to hand every employee a 300-dollar bonus check.

You're ecstatic. You've just had your car in the shop for a new power steering pump which cost you—you guessed it—299 dollars. You can't believe that the bonus could be so perfectly timed, and that it's just enough to cover the car repairs.

Back in your office, you notice that your co-worker, Celia, doesn't seem nearly as pleased about the bonus as you are.

"Wasn't the bonus a fantastic surprise?" you ask her excitedly.

"Big deal," is her reply. "I can't believe all this company could only come up with was a measley 300 dollars after all the work we've done this year."

*   *   *

You're a graphic artist. You've always felt that the most satisfying kind of work for you would be to illustrate children's books. Eventually, through a lot of hard work and persistence, you land a contract to illustrate a children's book by a promising new author.

When the book comes out, your family and friends are enthusiastic, proud and excited for you.

"Doesn't it feel great to see your work published like this?" your sister asks you.

"I could have done it better. It's okay, but I don't really feel like the illustrations are good enough," you answer.

*   *   *

What do all these situations have in common? Read them again and you'll see it.

Right—they all have to do with the question "How much is enough?"

In the first example above, you know you've had enough exercise when your body starts saying, "Help! Help!" However, your friend Terry is still ready for more. People's physical condition, their enjoyment of exercise and sports, and their level of desire to be more fit or more skilled all determine how much exercise is enough for them.

In the second example, you've decided you've had enough to eat because you feel full—but there's still cake and ice cream. Your mother doesn't feel that she's fed the family enough unless it's topped off with dessert. Her idea of what's enough food and yours are different.

The scenario with the 300-dollar bonus raises a question about how much money is enough. For you, the 300 dollars is enough of a bonus because it covers your recent car expenses. For your co-worker Celia, it's obviously not enough. But you wonder if perhaps Celia is the kind of person for whom nothing is ever enough.

Finally, the situation regarding the book illustrations deals with whether your work is good enough *and* what level of achievement is high enough. For years you thought that illustrating a book would represent the height of achievement for you, but then when it happens, you find fault with the work you did on the book instead of feeling that you've finally reached a major goal. What you thought would be enough in terms of your career aspirations apparently wasn't enough after all.

I think this issue of "How much is enough?" is a critical one as we continue our journey of success. Goals will play an important role in our journey. If we are to ever meet those goals, we'll need to decide what is enough in that specific area. If one of our goals is to spend more time with our children, for example, we need to have some sense of what is enough time, or else we'll feel like failures every time we leave for work or go to a meeting or attend a Bible study instead of being with our children.

How do we recognize enoughness when we attain it? Are there areas of our lives in which enoughness never happens? Inability to recognize enoughness can send us down paths of frustration and delay on our journey; learning when to say "This is enough" and when not to can help keep us moving forward.

How Much Is Enough?

Defining "enough" is hard. Think about what it would take for you to feel you had attained—

- "Enough" job accomplishment, authority, or responsibility
- "Enough" sense of self-worth
- "Enough" talent or ability
- "Enough" spiritual growth
- "Enough" knowledge.

Or how about these "enoughs"?

- "Enough" time and effort devoted to parenting
- "Enough" love and support given to your spouse
- "Enough" time and effort invested in your own personhood.

It's Just a Glass of Water

Picture a glass tumbler that contains half the amount of water needed to fill it.

Do you have the image in your mind? Okay, now answer this question: Is the glass half empty or half full?

You've undoubtedly heard this illustration before. It's often used to describe two kinds of people in the world: those who see the glass as half empty and those who see it as half full. The former group sees something lacking, something missing, something to be disappointed and discontented about. The latter group recognizes what is there; they see something to appreciate or be grateful for.

The illustration of the half-filled glass (I guess you can tell which group I fall into!) can teach us something important about "enoughness."

("Enoughness" is my own coined word and conveys a very important concept. If you are a stickler for semantics, you can substitute the word "sufficiency" if you like, although I don't like it nearly as well.)

There are four basic aspects of enoughness that I believe we need to explore. They are:

- Having enough
- Doing enough
- Being enough
- Knowing enough.

Let's look at these elements one at a time.

Having Enough

Like many other parts of the country, Florida has recently instituted a state-supported lottery. I voted against it, I still oppose it, and I don't play it—but that's not the point. The point is that the lottery makes it possible for people to become millionaires literally overnight. For the price of a one-dollar lottery ticket you could suddenly find yourself the recipient of five or ten or twenty million dollars, paid to you in installments of hundreds of thousands of dollars a year.

The possibility of such sudden wealth has prompted people to speculate on how they would spend those winnings. I think those speculations can tell us a great deal about ourselves.

For example, let's say you won a recent lottery jackpot of 8 million dollars. How would you spend it? Let your imagination run wild.

List the major purchases you would make:

(House? Car? Vacation home? Boat?)

_____

_____

_____

_____

_____

_____

Now list the things you would *do:*

(Take an around-the-world cruise? Spend the weekends at posh resorts? Rent a major tourist attraction for your own private birthday party?)

_____

_____

_____

_____

Finally, list the other things you would use the money for:

_____

_____

_____

_____

Now look back at your list. Do you think the items you listed would total more or less than 8 million dollars?

Here's where we get into the idea of "enoughness" as it pertains to material wealth. If the expenditures you listed above would come to less than 8 million dollars, then theoretically if you won the lottery jackpot you would have enough money for the things you desire. If, on the other hand, the items you listed would cost more than 8 million dollars, then what sounds like an infinitely large sum of money really isn't enough to obtain the things you want.

We're back to the question of whether the imaginary glass is half empty or half full. A person who wins the lottery might purchase all the things she wants or needs, and have money left over to invest for future income, insurance against medical bills, and other types of financial security. In other words, the 8-million-dollar jackpot would be enough.

By contrast, another person might spend every penny of the winnings on material desires and whims, and then feel deprived when the money runs out and she hasn't purchased or done all the things she wanted. The 8 million dollars wouldn't have been enough.

Obviously, how much material wealth is "enough" is different for each person. There's a popular expression that says, "You can't be too rich or too thin." While to my knowledge the Bible doesn't comment on the ideal waist size, it does clearly indicate that it is possible for a person to be "too rich"—that is, to have too much material wealth for his or her spiritual well-being.

That was the case with the rich young man whom Jesus encountered in Matthew 19. He was eager to follow all of God's commandments—*until* Jesus mentioned the part about giving away all his possessions. He just couldn't do it. I think one of the most heartrending passages in all of Scripture is Matthew 19:22, which tells us that this young man "went away sad, because he had great wealth." The tragedy lies in the choice the young man made: He chose to forgo salvation rather than part with his possessions. I believe he was indeed "too rich."

The Bible contains clear guidelines for helping us determine enoughness in relation to material wealth. The underlying principles seem to be these.

1. When earthly wealth—either the pursuit of it or the attainment of it—interferes with our walk with God and our obedience to Him, then we have passed the "enough" mark and moved into the range of "too much."

Paul discussed this danger in his first letter to his young friend Timothy. "People who want to get rich fall into temptation and a trap and into many foolish and harmful desires that plunge men into ruin and destruction. For the love of money is a root of all kinds of evil. Some people, eager for money, have wandered from the faith and pierced themselves with many griefs" (1 Timothy 6:9,10).

Possessions and riches are neither good nor evil in themselves. Like work and ambition, wealth is a resource, a tool for us to use. How we use it and what role we let it play in our lives determines whether its influence is good or evil. When it becomes a driving force in our lives, directing our decisions, affecting our relationships, leading us into immoral or unethical behavior, or causing us to compromise or sacrifice what God has entrusted to us—then the danger signals are up. We have let wealth become an idol, giving it the place of honor and influence that should be reserved for God alone. Any time material riches distract our focus from God's sovereignty and His commandments, our long-term spiritual welfare is in jeopardy.

"Turn my heart toward your statutes," the psalmist wrote, "and not toward selfish gain" (Psalm 119:36). There's that word "selfish" again. Just as when we talk about ambition, our motives are important when we evaluate our pursuit of wealth. Paul talks about "people who want to get rich," people who are "eager for money." These are the ones who bring temptation, grief, and ruin upon themselves. It is not our possessions or our money per se that cause these things, according to Paul, but "the *love* of money" that produces evil.

What motivates us in our pursuit of material wealth? Is it simply a desire to "get rich"? Is it a desire to have people admire or envy us? Is it a way to prove our own worth in a standard of measure that the world understands? Is our goal to provide opportunities and comforts for ourselves and our loved ones? To protect our own and our family's futures? To have more resources to do the work to which God has called us?

For you, where is the line between "enough" and "too much"?

2. Unless the accumulation of earthly possessions is accompanied by the accumulation of spiritual knowledge, the result can only be disaster.

SIGNPOST

A man who has riches
without understanding is like
the beasts that perish.

—Psalm 49:20

Throughout the Bible, God repeatedly warns us that it takes spiritual wisdom to successfully manage wealth rather than letting it manage us. In Luke 12 Jesus told the parable of the rich fool, a man who had such a good crop one year that he decided to build bigger barns to store it all. Then, he reasoned, he could sit back and take life easy, concentrating on his own pleasures. Here is the rest of the story:

"But God said to him, 'You fool! This very night your life will be demanded from you. Then who will get what you have prepared for yourself?'

"This is how it will be with anyone who stores up things for himself but is not rich toward God" (Luke 12:20,21).

Jesus warned that our hearts will follow our treasures; that is, what we value most is what will shape our choices, our decisions, and the course of our lives, both now and for eternity. That's why He urged us not to "store up . . . treasures on earth, where moth and rust destroy, and where thieves break in and steal. But store up for yourselves treasures in heaven. . . . For where your treasure is, there your heart will be also" (Matthew 6:19-21).

Every day the world tells us that earthly wealth should be our goal, that we should be storing up earthly treasures. We are bombarded with communications that urge us to desire and obtain more, more, more. Each of us receives bushels of mail proposing get-rich techniques and schemes, better ways to multiply our money, and strategies for obtaining possessions that we can't really afford. The world is constantly luring us away from the pursuit of spiritual riches and encouraging us to pursue material ones. It's a very persuasive message, and one that takes increasing spiritual fortitude to withstand.

In order to handle the temptations of material wealth—whether those temptations arise from desiring it or from having it—we need to be "rich toward God"—that is, spiritually strong enough, obedient enough, and mature enough to maintain our focus on God's commandments and not be sidetracked into focusing on earthly desires. The greater the wealth, the greater the temptations, and the greater spiritual strength we need.

3. The contrast between earthly gain and spiritual gain is the difference between the temporary and the eternal.

Of all the biblical themes about wealth, this is one of the most recurrent. The temporary nature of earthly life is a fundamental principle of resurrection theology. "I am a stranger on earth," the psalmist wrote (Psalm 119:19). We discussed this same principle at the end of the last chapter in relation to work and ambition. We are strangers here, sojourners in a foreign land; we are not permanent residents. The things that are of value by this world's standards will not be of value in the place where we will spend eternity. We cannot take with us the material gains we accumulate in this life—only the spiritual ones.

When we find ourselves being caught up in the ambition-work-wealth cycle, a simple reminder to ourselves about the temporary nature of these things can effectively snap us back to reality.

In October of 1988 I had the opportunity to spend a weekend in beautiful Charleston, South Carolina. The city's colorful, picturesque homes, the residents' fierce and protective pride in their city's history, the careful and loving preservation of the area's natural beauty and historical value—all left me feeling inspired and uplifted.

A year later, in the wake of Hurricane Hugo, I saw a newspaper photo of an area I had walked through several times during my visit to Charleston. In the photo, what had been a picturesque spot on a historic street was no more than a pile of gray rubble.

As if the rampant devastation caused by Hurricane Hugo weren't an adequate reminder of the impermanence of material things, a few weeks later an earthquake brought scores of deaths and immeasurable havoc to the people of the San Francisco vicinity. Like the biblical character Job, many of the individuals affected by these disasters lost everything, regardless of what kind of lives they had lived until then, how hard they had worked, or how successful they had become. How easily and how quickly "treasures on earth" can be lost!

4. To learn "contentment" should be one of our goals.

Contentment is closely allied to enoughness. Contentment isn't the same thing as happiness; it has more to do with inner peace, an absence of striving. It's the ability to be at peace with where you are, with what you have, and with how you're living at any given time. It doesn't mean giving up or settling for second-best; it's not resignation or hopelessness, nor does it mean we've abandoned our goals. We can be content and still be growing; in fact, contentment frees up more time and energy for growth because it keeps us from wearing ourselves out pursuing unimportant things.

"But godliness with contentment is great gain," Paul wrote. "For we brought nothing into the world, and we can take nothing out of it. But if we have food and clothing, we will be content with that" (1 Timothy 6:6,7).

How much does it take for us to be content? An 8-million-dollar lottery prize? A new car? A salary that's double our present one?

I believe that one secret to contentment is learning to see the glass as half-full. Remember Celia, your co-worker whom we met in the scenario at the beginning of this chapter? I don't think a person like Celia will ever be content, because she'll spend her life complaining that the glass is half-empty. We cannot experience contentment if we see only what is missing in our lives.

Ellen, a friend of mine who has been divorced for several years, was talking about a friend of hers, also divorced, who lives in another city. Ellen had just spent a weekend visiting her.

"She's just convinced," Ellen said of her friend, "that if she finds another husband, her life will be perfect. She's focusing all her energies on that goal. It's like, if she gets married again, then she'll be happy.

"After being with her, and seeing how discontented she is being single, I realized that I just have to accept that I may not get married again. Yes, I'd like to—but that may not happen, and if I keep seeing my life as lacking and unsatisfactory because I'm not married, then I'll never be happy. I don't want to live like that. I want to like my life the way it is. If I find someone and get married, great. But I don't want to wait for that to happen before I can be happy."

Ellen had seen that her friend was focusing on what was missing in her life. As a result, Ellen decided to practice contentment, to focus on her life *as it is* rather than on how she would like it to be different. This doesn't mean that she has to stop hoping for change, but it can help her avoid living in a state of constant discontent until that change occurs.

We don't know what God has in store for us, but He asks us to trust Him to meet our needs. When we learn to trust Him, we can practice contentment. We can certainly still work to make our lives better, but in the process we can know that He is in control and that we will have what we need. Contentment means being at peace with both where we are and where we're headed.

The apostle Paul described contentment this way: "I know what it is to be in need, and I know what it is to have plenty. I have learned the secret of being content in any and every situation, whether well-fed or hungry, whether living in plenty or in want. I can do everything through him who gives me strength" (Philippians 4:12,13).

SIGNPOST

*Do not be overawed
when a man grows rich,
when the splendor
of his house increases;
for he will take nothing with him
when he dies,
his splendor will not descend with him.*

—Psalm 49:16,17

Doing Enough

In the last chapter we talked about work as an idol. One of the realities that fosters work-as-idolatry is the fact that our society admires *doing*. It rewards attainment, accomplishment, achievement. That's not necessarily bad; after all, it's much easier to measure and to see what people have *done* than what they *are*, and people certainly deserve to be recognized for hard work, dedicated service, or outstanding performance.

But sometimes this emphasis on doing can cause us to make unrealistic demands on ourselves. Consider Rosemary, a new mother who's still adjusting to life at home with a two-month-old baby.

Here's how she feels:

"I saw a bumper sticker the other day that said, 'Of all the things I've lost, I miss my mind the most.' When I saw that, I thought, *I have to get one of those. That's exactly how I feel!*

"I worked outside the home for eight years before my daughter Jackie was born. At the end of my workday I could always look back and see what I'd accomplished. But now, at the end of the day I feel like I haven't done anything, yet I'm still exhausted! The house looks like it's been ransacked. I haven't written a letter to my mother in weeks. My husband's laundry and my own is turning into a mountain; the baby is the only one in the family who has clean clothes.

"But I'm so tired that all I want to do is take a nap. I know I've burned up a lot of energy all day, but I sure don't have anything to show for it. When Don comes home from work and asks me what I did today, it seems like I always say 'I don't know.' Sometimes I really do feel like I'm losing my mind."

In reality, Rosemary has spent the day caring for an infant—a demanding job if there ever was one. Yet she doesn't feel that this is enough to show for her day. She has in her mind, whether she's aware of it or not, a standard of what's "enough" work for one day, and she feels she's not measuring up, not doing enough.

Most of us who are mothers can identify with this feeling, especially if we worked outside the home before the baby came along. Suddenly there was a drastic change in our ability to do "enough" to make us feel that we had put in a productive and worthwhile day.

Even working women who aren't mothers deal with this issue of doing enough. We work outside the home all day, then come home to garages that need cleaning, laundry that needs doing, faucets that need repairing, buttons to be sewn on, carpets to be vacuumed, bathrooms to be cleaned, refrigerators to be filled, meals to be fixed. Whether we're married or not, and whether our spouse does or doesn't help around the house, our homes echo with little voices that say, "Clean me!" "Fix me!" "Scrub me!" "Mend me!" "Sort me!" "Mail me!"

Working women receive conflicting messages from the world around them regarding what's "enough" for them to be doing. Is it enough to attain a position of responsibility and prestige in your career, or do you have to be able to turn out a five-star dinner as well? Is it enough to have a warm, welcoming home, or do you have to be able to manage a quarter-million-dollar advertising budget too? Is it enough to have well-adjusted, well-groomed, capable children, or only if they're Presidential Scholars? Is it enough to attain a supervisory position, or do you have to become a department head? Is it enough to be a department head, or do you have to become a director?

Is it enough to attend the performance of your child's school play, or is it necessary that you stitch up an angel costume too? Is attending your son's baseball games enough, or only if you're the team mother also?

Is accompanying your spouse to his company's Christmas party enough, or do you have to fix all the hors d'oeuvres too?

The question of how much is enough crops up virtually every day as we go about our busy lives. Whether we're willing to accept it or not, the fact is that we can't do it all. There's simply more out there for each of us to do than one person can complete. How do we decide what's enough? Or do we just keep taking on more and more, trying to do it all, until we crash and burn?

I think a key to recognizing enoughness in regard to our doing lies in understanding *limits*. In some areas of our lives we need to be willing to set our own limits and/ or to accept the existing limitations of time, energy, material resources, circumstances, and other factors. In other areas of our lives, I believe we need to maintain a state of "willing dissatisfaction"—that is, a confident and optimistic willingness to continually reach beyond what we have already done.

Cindy and her husband, Dan, recently opened a group of small businesses in my neighborhood, including a restaurant, a take-out pizza place, a yogurt shop, and a video rental business. On any given day, one or both of them can be found working in one of the businesses, although they have a number of other employees as well. Cindy and I were talking yesterday about how difficult it is to decide how much time and effort is enough to invest in their businesses, particularly in light of the fact that the couple also has two school-aged children.

"It's not like we can say, 'Well, we've done enough business for this month. Let's close up and take a few weeks off,' " she said. "I just don't think we could do that."

I asked her how she sets limits for herself in regard to how much is "enough" time for her to devote to the businesses.

"I go by gut instinct," she told me. "I try to decide how much of my being gone the kids can handle. If I feel like it's getting to be too much, I back off. The kids have always been my first priority." In other words, Cindy is willing to set limits on the time she spends on the business in order to accommodate a higher priority—even though she admits that, if she let it, the business could consume 24 hours a day for both herself and her husband.

How much is enough in regard to the things we do for our children? How good a job do we do on setting limits there?

"I'm not very good at that," Cindy admits. "I always go overboard. I haven't managed to achieve much balance."

Child-rearing is a good example of an area in which we need to think carefully about limits, deciding where limits are applicable and where they aren't. I believe that we need to set realistic limits on the things we do for our children based on the reality that our time, energy, and physical capacity are limited.

We don't like to admit this, but we need to make time to take care of ourselves. We need to eat adequately, sleep a reasonable amount, get enough exercise to keep our bodies from deteriorating, and in other ways maintain our physical selves. We also need to pay attention to our emotional, intellectual, and spiritual needs. Yet these needs of ours are the first to be disregarded when our time and energy start to be spread too thin.

I believe that constantly trying to do more for our children at the expense of even the most minimal personal well-being is counterproductive. Staying up all night to be sure our child has 12 dozen cookies for the third-grade Easter party reflects either faulty planning or an unwillingness to set limits on what we can do. Missing Bible study every week in order to pick up a child at ballet or soccer practice, instead of arranging to carpool occasionally, seems like going past the limits of enoughness.

Recently my son told me in detail of the elaborate costume that his friend Nate's mother, Debby, was sewing for her son to wear to the school's fall costume party. This particular mother happens to be a veteran seamstress who has her own home-sewing business. Hearing the trace of envy and admiration in my son's voice as he described the costume, I would have loved to be able to say, "Would you like a costume like that? I'll make you one if you do." But there's no way in the world I could make a costume like that. For one thing, I don't have the skill, and for another, even if I were willing to stay up all night for a week, I still wouldn't have time. (Debby, on the other hand, can probably make it in one evening.) I can either accept those limitations or else carry around a burdensome sense of guilt and failure. I choose to do the former.

There is always an unlimited number of tasks for us to accomplish at any given time. Even if we could come to a point where we felt we had done enough for our families, our spouses, our jobs, and ourselves (which isn't likely to happen), there is still a world out there with a diversity of desperate needs. Our churches need us. Our communities need us. The homeless, the hungry, the disenfranchised, the disabled, the elderly—they need us to do many things they cannot do for themselves. Yet because we are human, we cannot do it all, and so the task becomes one of choosing carefully what we *will* do.

On what basis do we make choices about how to invest the limited resources of time and energy available to us? This brings us back to the question we discussed in the last section, the question of where our heart is. Our decisions about what we will do—and what will be enough—will be directed by what is important to us. The Bible is full of clear and practical guidelines for making these decisions.

For example, regarding the pursuit of wealth: "Do not wear yourself out to get rich; have the wisdom to show restraint" (Proverbs 23:4). Now that's a pretty clear statement about setting limits on how much we're willing to do in pursuit of material gain!

Regarding the rearing of children, the Bible does not once mention baking large quantities of cookies or hosting elaborate birthday parties as criteria for good parenting. Instead, it speaks of the teaching role of parents: "Fix these words of mine in your hearts and minds. . . . Teach them to your children" (Deuteronomy 11:18,19). There are limits to how much of the busy-ness of rearing children we can realistically handle at any given time. But I don't believe there is a limit to how much effort we can devote to teaching our children the things of God. I think this is one of the areas in which we need to maintain the state of "willing dissatisfaction" I mentioned earlier: constantly seeking better ways to communicate and exemplify God's message to our children.

Similarly, the realities of the clock and the calendar limit how much we can physically accomplish to feed the hungry, shelter the homeless, befriend the lonely, and meet all the other needs of people in our world. Certainly we need to do what we can. By identifying where our time and talent are most needed, and then setting reasonable limits on what we commit to doing, we can maximize the effectiveness of our efforts.

But is there a limit on kindness or compassion or concern? Is there a limit on supporting others in prayer? Is there a limit to graciousness of spirit, to love, to joy? We need to abide by the limits of what we can *do*, but not on what we can *be*. (We'll talk more about "being" later in this chapter.)

That Sister of Mine!

The biblical sisters Mary and Martha teach us a critical lesson about doing. Here is the story which the Gospel writer Luke tells about these two women:

"As Jesus and his disciples were on their way, he came to a village where a woman named Martha opened her home to him. She had a sister called Mary, who sat at the Lord's feet listening to what he said. But Martha was distracted by all the preparations that had to be made. She came to him and asked, 'Lord, don't you care that my sister has left me to do the work by myself? Tell her to help me!'

"'Martha, Martha,' the Lord answered, 'you are worried and upset about many things, but only one thing is needed. Mary has chosen what is better, and it will not be taken away from her' " (Luke 10:38-41).

Can you identify with Martha? I can.

She's a doer. We can easily picture her bustling around, fixing food, making sure the serving dishes are full and that everyone has enough to drink, straightening a rug, moving a chair, and shooing stray dogs or children out of the open doorway lest they disturb the Master and his companions. After all, a Very Important Person is visiting her home, and she's anxiously checking and rechecking to make sure everything is just right.

How irritated she would be to see that her sister, Mary, isn't helping a bit. That Mary! Just sitting there listening to Jesus talk as if there weren't a single task to be done!

Yet Jesus told Martha that her sister had "chosen what is better."

I'm afraid there is often too much Martha and too little Mary in each of us. Perhaps what we need is a balance between Martha's industriousness and Mary's spiritual attentiveness. Like Martha, we become consumed by the overwhelming number of tasks to be done and we fail to take time for spiritual growth and personal enrichment.

Imagine—Martha had Jesus *right there* in her home, where she could reach out and touch Him, where she could ask Him anything she wanted, where she could see firsthand what this revolutionary preacher was really like—and yet she occupied herself with household tasks! Her sister Mary chose instead to seize the opportunity to hear, to learn, to experience a divine presence as few were privileged to do.

It scares me that in my own frantic doing I also might miss such an opportunity. I pray that God would teach me to know when I have done enough, so that I don't neglect "what is better."

In giving us free will, God gave us the responsibility for making choices about what we will do with the resources He gives us. Determining not only how we will use those resources but how much "doing" is enough in each area of our lives is part of that decision-making process. And it's not easy. The competition for our time, energy, and attention is staggering. The challenge to us is to be selective, to know when we have done enough and when there is more to be done, to know where to set limits and where to refuse to set them.

Being Enough

I believe that one of the reasons working women have so much difficulty setting limits on "doing" is that we haven't learned how to do a very good job of "being." We have become confused about who we are, and that has produced the confusion about what we should be doing. Should we be corporate executives? Nobel prize winners? Homemakers? All three? Or should we strive to be persons of compassion, insight, selflessness, and wisdom, regardless of what we "do"?

Unfortunately, our society doesn't recognize "being" nearly as much as doing—which is understandable, because it's harder to see. Beth, who is the vice-president of a local bank, summed this up well. She was talking about the two-year period she took off from her job at the time her daughter was born.

"I learned just how much my job was tied up with my identity," she said. "I found out it's a lot more comfortable to say, 'Hi, I'm Beth, vice-president of XYZ Bank,' than 'Hi, I'm Beth . . . .' " We find it so much easier to talk about ourselves in terms of what we *do* than in terms of what we *are*. Perhaps it's because we feel that, while our accomplishments and activities may be worthwhile, we by ourselves are not. This chronic sense of inadequacy, according to Scripture, isn't what God intended for us, but it's still very prevalent in our world.

My friend and co-worker Bob Kelly, a social worker with a PhD in counseling, has given a great deal of thought to this sense of never "being enough." In one of his poems, entitled "Some of the Pain," Bob talks about how much this chronic sense of inadequacy can hurt:

"How can it be
that when
I'm all I can be
I'm not enough?

Some of the pain
is believing
that if I would do just a little more
it would be enough
and because I can't
I am inadequate—
not enough.

Some of the pain
of not being enough
is the pain of feeling rejected,
devalued,
of not being loved
because
I'm not enough!

I must learn
that another's dissatisfaction
is a statement
about them,
not about me.[1]

Why is it that we so often feel inadequate? I believe it is because we simply do not have a firm and deep-seated sense of our own inherent value as human beings, a sense of worth and importance separate from our occupation, our identity as employees or spouses or mothers, our material possessions, our surroundings, or our personal history.

God created us with the capability of being like Him. He gave us dominion over the world and all the things in it. He allowed His Son—in fact, *sent* Him—to die so that we could realize the fullness of life as His children. And yet we continue to believe that we are of value only when we accomplish something or attain something. We have failed to hear what God is telling us. We have failed to acknowledge the reality of His grace.

In one sense we *are* inadequate. By ourselves we cannot attain the perfection of Christ's example. We cannot completely resist the temptations to which our human nature makes us subject. But with the assurance of God's grace and forgiveness, we can be confident of our worth in His sight in spite of our shortcomings.

Yes, God expects us to do the work of advancing His kingdom on earth, spreading the gospel, bringing His love to a torn and unloving world, but what we do or don't do isn't the basis for His love or for our worth.

I believe that many Christians misunderstand the nature of God's grace. They feel that because they aren't perfect, they're failing God.

I lost my temper yesterday at work. The office was extremely busy and I was rushing to leave because I had another appointment to go to. Five minutes before I was to walk out the door, someone reminded me that I hadn't written an article that had to be turned in by the end of the day. I was furious with myself for forgetting and not having the article done, and a (small) show of temper erupted before I got a grip on myself.

I wish that hadn't happened. I know it made the person who reminded me about the article uncomfortable, it embarrassed me, and it certainly wasn't a very good testimony to my faith. But I'm human. It happened. I'm not perfect, and God knows it. He loves me anyway, and He'll forgive me. I am not a failure in God's sight simply because I failed to control my temper yesterday.

Perhaps it's because Christ, our model and example, is perfect that we feel we have to be, even though Scripture is clear that God doesn't demand that of us. Because Christ was selfless, we want to be selfless too. Because He was infinitely loving to even the most unlovable men and women, we want to be that way too. Because He was patient, wise, and understanding, we feel that we should demonstrate those qualities to the nth degree also.

Are you selfless, loving, patient, wise, and understanding 100 percent of the time? I'm not. Christ was human, like we are. But He was also divine. He was capable of a perfection of which we are not fully capable on this earth. I believe it's a realistic goal for us to desire, with God's help, to be *more like* Christ, and to constantly model our lives after Him. I don't believe it's realistic for us to punish ourselves when we fail to measure up to His perfect standard. God doesn't; He forgives. He doesn't write us off for "not being enough." His grace is His gift to us, His assurance that He loves us even though we're not perfect.

I believe that our sense of inadequacy also stems from our desire to meet *other* people's expectatons. In his poem Bob Kelly says, "I must learn/that another's dissatisfaction/is a statement about them/not about me."

What other people think is important to us; their opinion of us matters. In the workplace, at home, at church—in fact anyplace we go—we have to be able to get along with others, to effectively maintain that delicate chemistry which enables people to live and work together. But our goal in life, according to the Bible, is not to be what other people think we should be; it's to be what God designed us to be. "For you created my inmost being," the psalmist wrote, "you knit me together in my mother's womb. . . . All the days ordained for me were written in your book before one of them came to be" (Psalm 139:13,16).

Naturally, we want to please the people who are important to us. At the age of nearly 40, I still find myself eagerly trying to please my mother. And certainly I want my husband and son, and my sister, and my employer, and others whose opinions are important to me, to be happy with who I am and not be disappointed in me. However, I need to accept the fact that I can't always please them, and I also need to acknowledge that their expectations may not always be the right ones for me. Furthermore, others' expectations are not always in keeping with what God desires for us; sometimes we have to choose between the two.

One of the joys of relying on God's Word as our guideline for "being" is that it's always right, always true, always what's best for us. Human beings, on the other hand, make mistakes, errors in judgment, and decisions based on personal motives. Our friends', employers', and loved ones' expectations of us may change over time, reflecting what those individuals need from us at any given moment. In contrast, God's desires and goals for us remain constant throughout time and into eternity. If the goal of our "being" is to please Him, then we can be sure of being "enough."

Knowing Enough

Is it possible to know enough about any given subject? For example:

• You're running late for work. You race out to your car, start it, and hear an ominous "ka-brump, ka-brump" coming from somewhere under the hood. Visions of a three-digit mechanic's bill pass through your mind. Do you wish you knew more about cars?

• You're scheduled to leave on a business trip to Seattle on Tuesday. It's Sunday evening. Your throat feels like it's been sandpapered, the room swirls every time you stand up, and your whole body argues with you when you try to move. You wonder if Tuesday night will find you frantically flipping through the Seattle yellow pages to find a doctor's office that's open. Do you wish you knew more about health?

• Your teenage son has been sulky and uncommunicative lately. Last night he skipped dinner, saying he wasn't hungry, then proceeded to eat a whole bag of chocolate bars followed by a double cheeseburger. He received a telephone call—which you answered—from a young lady who politely asked you to "tell him I hope the dog eats his football jersey." Do you wish you knew more about adolescent psychology?

How much knowledge is enough? How much do we need to know to do our jobs effectively? How much do we need to know to get along with other people? How much do we need to know to be good parents, spouses, citizens?

Our era has been characterized as the Information Age. The axiom that "knowledge is power" has probably never been more true than it is today. The whirlwind development of new technology causes change in the world at a head-spinning pace. It feels like a full-time job just to stay abreast of the most basic information necessary for survival: which foods cause cancer (all of them, it seems); what lethal gases might be leaking into our houses; what animals and insects carry potentially fatal disease germs; what secret subcultures are plotting strategies to brainwash us; what evil influences threaten our children; what destructive psychological ploys are being used by special-interest groups to manipulate our thinking.

At the same time, new information is being thrust at us constantly as the media intrude more and more into our lives. It's easy to feel overwhelmed by the sheer volume of information that we need to process and absorb each day.

Again we face the challenge of selectivity and limit-setting, of choosing how much knowledge is enough, and what we need most to know. I doubt seriously that we can ever know enough, if only because life is too fast-changing and too unpredictable.

As a high school and college student, I was confident I would never need to know anything about physics. That attitude changed on the day, as a young reporter, I interviewed William Lear, creator of the Learjet. I doubt that I understood one-tenth of what the renowned inventor said, because I simply didn't have the necessary background knowledge. That was the day I became convinced that there's no such thing as too much knowledge.

Even as there is probably no upper limit to the amount of earthly knowledge we can accumulate or use, I believe there is also a certain minimum of spiritual knowledge that we need to have if we are to live the lives to which God calls us. This threefold base of knowledge includes 1) knowing who God is, 2) knowing what He has done, both historically and spiritually, and 3) knowing His expectations for the way we live our lives.

Without this base of knowledge, no other knowledge, no experience, no activity, no relationship will have any meaning. God made us in His image; surely we cannot begin to understand ourselves if we do not try to learn as much as we can about Him (accepting as we do so that a full understanding of Him is beyond our grasp). Unless we have some inkling of divine perspective, we will constantly struggle to make sense of what occurs in and around us.

The Bible, of course, is our primary source of this knowledge. It reveals God to us by recording His work in the collective life of mankind from the time of creation. It tells us His message as spoken through those whom He has chosen throughout history. It spells out for us the way He expects us to live in relation to Him and to those around us.

The Holy Spirit is another source of this knowledge. Jesus promised His disciples, as he promises us, that the Holy Spirit, the Counselor, "will teach you all things and will remind you of everything I have said to you" (John 14:26).

Like the importance of work, the importance of knowledge is firmly established in Scripture. However, the Bible makes it equally clear that knowledge alone is not enough to make the man or woman of God complete. The apostle Paul wrote in 1 Corinthians 13 that knowledge without love is worthless. Peter, in his second letter to the Asian churches, encouraged believers to "make every effort to add to your... knowledge, self-control; and to self-control, perseverance; and to perseverance, godliness; and to godliness, brotherly kindness, and to brotherly kindness, love" (2 Peter 1:5-7). In addition, biblical references to knowledge are often accompanied by references to wisdom, insight, discernment, and understanding, all of which are important complements to knowledge.

Obviously knowledge, either earthly or heavenly, is only another resource, another tool that God makes available to us as we seek to fulfill His plan and do the unique work to which He calls us. Because God is infinite and our minds are not, it is impossible for us ever to acquire enough knowledge of Him. Equally impossible is succeeding in any real and lasting sense on the basis of knowledge alone.

Also because God is infinite, the concept of "enoughness" doesn't apply to Him. He is sufficient in every way. But we as human beings live in a world of limits—limits to having, doing, being, and knowing. Our lifelong challenge is to determine when setting limits—defining enoughness—can help us in our journey of success, and when our best course is to rely on the unlimited resources of God.

POINTS OF INTEREST

1. In what aspects of your life do you feel you have attained "enoughness"? List some examples below.

_____

_____

_____

_____

2. In what areas of your life do you feel you'll never be able to say, "This is enough"?

_____

_____

_____

_____

_____

3. In this chapter we discussed a) having enough, b) doing enough, c) being enough, and d) knowing enough. In which of these areas is it hardest for you to define enoughness?

4. In regard to "doing enough," list a) one facet of your life in which you would like to set more limits, and b) one in which you would like to remain "willingly dissatisfied."

a) _____

b) _____

5. What can you do, starting today, to make the changes suggested by a) and b) above?

_____

_____

_____

_____

6. How is the balance between the Martha and the Mary in you? In what ways would you like to change it?

_____

_____

_____

7. When you evaluate whether you are "being enough" in some relationship or activity in your life, whose expectations are most influential in your evaluation?

_____

_____

_____

8. How extensive is your "basic knowledge" about God in each of these areas?

   a) Who God is.

_____
No knowledge   Much knowledge

   b) What God has done.

_____
No knowledge   Much knowledge

   c) What God expects.

_____
No knowledge   Much knowledge

190 / *When Enough Is Enough*

9. What steps will you take to increase your knowledge in the three areas above?

_____

_____

_____

_____

SIGNPOST

*Keep your lives free from the love of money
and be content with what you have,
because God has said, "Never will I
leave you; never will I forsake you."*

—Hebrews 13:5

*Trust in the Lord with all your heart
and lean not on your own understanding;
in all your ways acknowledge him,
and he will make your paths straight.*

—Proverbs 3:5,6

*This righteousness from God
comes through faith in Jesus Christ
to all who believe . . . . for all have sinned
and fall short of the glory of God,
and are justified freely by his grace
through the redemption that came
by Christ Jesus.*

—Romans 3:22-24

CHAPTER 10

What Does It Take to Get There?

Character cannot be developed
in ease and quiet. Only through experience
of trial and suffering
can the soul be strengthened,
vision cleared, ambition inspired,
and success achieved.

—Helen Keller

HELP WANTED

Field Laborers: Needed for demanding, diversified work in worldwide corporation. Must be a hard worker, willing to put in long hours. Salary unrelated to credentials or experience. Requirements: courage; a willing heart; thankfulness; perseverance; hope. Employee benefits include job security, profit-sharing program, orientation manual, continuing education program, pension plan. Additional fringe benefits include wisdom, love, joy, peace, gentleness, meekness, faith, goodness. Apply in person. Equal opportunity employer.

*   *   *

Sounds like a pretty challenging job. Do you think you have what it takes?

What *does* it take to succeed as a woman of God? What is the "right stuff" that will enable us to meet our goal of living the lives God wants for us? As we progress on this journey toward success, what qualities of heart and spirit should we be learning, cultivating, and practicing? In short, what is God's formula for success?

I believe that just as God works in each of our lives uniquely and individually, His formula for success is different for each of us also. Our strengths and weaknesses, our backgrounds and histories, our likes and dislikes, our psychological makeup and personality quirks are all part of the formula that equals success in God's kingdom. Each of us can—and should—spend a lifetime studying His Word to learn the nature and extent of His standards for us. Only then can we understand how we can best serve Him in our own unique and individual way.

On the other hand, the Bible illustrates for us a number of qualities that have been demonstrated by God's people throughout the ages. Some of the most challenging among these are:

- Courage
- A willing heart
- Thankfulness
- Perseverance
- Hope

Surely a person with all those qualities could accomplish anything! Let's explore each of them and look at how we might build them into our own lives.

Going Where Angels Fear to Tread

The screech of tires outside was loud, sudden, and jarring. It was followed by a crash of metal on metal and splintering glass. My husband and I were playing a board game with another couple, Dave and Cynthia, at our home that evening. The sounds made it clear that a car accident had just occurred in the street outside our front door.

Cynthia, who is a nurse, ran to the window and looked out. "It looks pretty bad," she said. "I'm going out and see if I can help."

She came back a few minutes later, her hands covered with blood. "The paramedics are here," she told us. "It wasn't too bad. The driver had a scalp wound, and they always bleed a lot," she added as we looked, horrified, at her bloody hands. "I guess I'd better wash up if we're going to finish our game!"

It's been nearly 15 years since that accident occurred. What has stayed so clearly imprinted in my mind about that evening is Cynthia's immediate response to a situation in which someone needed help. It was dark when the accident occurred, and we couldn't see clearly enough to know exactly what the situation was in the street in front of our house. For all we knew, there could have been a gasoline spill just waiting for a spark to turn it into an explosion. There could have been a mangled body or a hysterical passenger, or both, in the car. A passing driver, unprepared to stop, could have crashed into the disabled car and injured anyone near it.

Cynthia didn't weigh all the possibilities before she went out into the street. She knew that someone was likely to need help, and she simply went.

Was Cynthia successful, in the traditional sense, in her career as a nurse? I don't know. I never observed her in her role at the hospital where she worked. I don't know if she was conscientious about completing paperwork, accurate in evaluating patients' conditions, punctual about schedules, obliging to her co-workers, and respectful of her supervisors' authority. But I know that on the night of that car accident Cynthia struck me as a woman of courage, and I believe we need courage if we are to succeed in God's kingdom.

We seldom talk about courage in our day-to-day lives, yet I see it around me constantly. I see my friend Paula facing life with courage and faith after the sudden death of her 31-year-old husband; I see Alice starting over after the pain of a divorce and saying, "I know God will get me through this. I'm learning to depend more on Him." I see Sandy, still loving an alcoholic husband, but moving out with her children to create a more stable and less violent home life for them.

In the working world, I see women standing up for the needs of the family against the pressures of career advancement; I see them refusing to participate in practices that skirt around ethics or foster a sexually charged work environment. I see them making courageous choices, forgoing material rewards in favor of other priorities and values.

I see women fighting against immoral or amoral value systems that threaten to take over our schools. I see them standing up and speaking out for those who cannot speak for themselves—the unborn, the disabled, the impoverished, the illiterate.

The courage of women who served in our Armed Forces during the Vietnam War is just now being recognized, along with that of the men who served beside them. But courage isn't always demonstrated in times of crises or physical danger. Sometimes, as with the biblical heroine Ruth, we're called to demonstrate quiet courage.

Ruth faced uncertainty and danger rather than abandon her widowed mother-in-law, Naomi. Picture her as a stranger in a foreign country, a solitary figure gathering grain in the fields to feed herself and Naomi. Hard physical labor, an inferior alien status, the dangers of being a woman alone—these were the circumstances of her daily life. Her courage was the day-to-day kind, the kind that enables a person to greet each day, whatever hardships or difficulties it might hold, with confidence and optimism.

In most Scripture references where courage is mentioned, it is in this context: "Be strong and courageous" (Deuteronomy 31:6,7,23; Joshua 1:6,7,9; 10:25; 2 Chronicles 32:7). Courage needs strength to back it up strength to withstand opposition, to face the unknown, to rebound from setbacks, to resist despair, to conquer frustration and discouragement. It takes strength to maintain a position when it's unpopular or when you're simply outnumbered.

In our journey to attain success in God's sight, we will encounter obstacles, roadblocks that seem to make further progress toward our goal impossible. We'll face temptations, risks, opposition, and difficult decisions with painful consequences. We'll ask ourselves if it's worth it; we'll wonder if we can ever reach that far-off goal. At times we may even wonder if God is still with us, or if somehow He has abandoned us or failed us. We'll despair because we feel inadequate—not good enough, not smart enough, not capable enough, not strong enough.

Perhaps that's why God's Word, through the example of great men and women of God, calls us to courage. He knows we'll need it if we're to succeed for Him.

SIGNPOST

Have I not commanded you?
Be strong and courageous.
Do not be terrified; do not be discouraged,
for the Lord your God will be with you
wherever you go.

—Joshua 1:9

The Spirit Is Willing—I Think

When my friend Cynthia became aware of the car accident described earlier, she not only showed the courage to plunge into an unknown situation, but she also had the willingness to take action. One without the other wouldn't have been very effective or very helpful to the injured driver. Scripture suggests that a willing heart is important for the servant of God who wants to succeed in His kingdom.

When Moses called the Israelites together to build the glorious tabernacle for God, as described in the book of Exodus, he summoned the best, most skilled artisans and craftspeople to do the work. He brought together goldsmiths, carpenters, engravers, weavers, tapestry designers, tanners to prepare the skins, and numerous others to put their abilities to work for God in this very special way. He wanted the best that human skill could produce to be reflected in this structure that would honor God.

Skill wasn't the only qualification of those who came to work on the tabernacle, though. Not every local artisan participated. The biblical account repeatedly emphasizes that only certain people came. Which ones?

"And everyone who was willing, and whose heart moved him came and brought an offering to the LORD for the work on the Tent of Meeting" (Exodus 35:21).

Talent and skill, and even courage, aren't enough to make us succeed by God's standards, whether in the world of work or in God's kingdom. Only when they are coupled with a willing heart can we move toward our spiritual destination. A young woman named Susan who works in our office constantly demonstrates the evidence of a willing heart. She's always the first to say, "Can I help?" or "Do you want me to take care of it?"

Yesterday I asked Susan if she knew where I could look up a certain bit of information I needed. As soon as I explained what I was looking for, she said, "I'll look it up for you," and she did. Often, in passing, I overhear her talking on the phone with people who are making inquiries of our office. I'm sure that the sincere concern and genuine helpfulness in her voice reveal her willing spirit even over the telephone.

A willing heart is closely allied to a spirit of servanthood. It disregards self-interest and power politics and seeks to reach out, to help, to support.

Of course, we have our limitations. Jesus knew that sometimes a willing spirit can be overcome by human weaknesses: "The spirit is willing, but the body is weak" (Matthew 26:41). Sometimes we have a willing spirit but lack the courage to do what needs to be done, or perhaps the lure of earthly temptations or the possibility of failure is too strong for us. I find it reassuring to know that Jesus understands these human shortcomings. But He still calls us to follow Him, to do the work that God has chosen us to do, "not because you must, but because you are willing, as God wants you to be; not greedy for money, but eager to serve . . . " (1 Peter 5:2).

A Note of Thanks

Remember the exercise class I mentioned in an earlier chapter? One of the things I enjoy most about it is the Christian fellowship, including the prayer the teacher gives at the end of each class. The theme of that prayer is always thankfulness. The prayer is usually along these lines:

"God, thank You for allowing us to be here today. We thank You for good health and strength, and we pray that we may always use these gifts to Your glory.

"We thank You for this country, Lord, and for the privilege of living in it and the freedom to worship You. We pray for those class members who are ill or are having a difficult time in some area of their lives; be with them and strengthen them. In Jesus' name, Amen."

We take so much for granted. We all need constant reminders of the many things we have for which to be grateful—our families; good health; the blessing of freedom; the community of faith; satisfying work; talents and skills that bring us pleasure and a sense of fulfillment. How often do we remember to thank God for them?

The apostle Paul gives us an inspiring model of thankfulness. If ever a person had ups and downs in life, it was this volatile, energetic, never-say-die evangelist. Here, in his own words, are some of his experiences: "I have labored and toiled and have often gone without sleep; I have known hunger and thirst and have often gone without food; I have been cold and naked" (2 Corinthians 11:27). In addition, we know that Paul was also beaten, imprisoned, persecuted, and defamed, all in Christ's name—yet he constantly thanked God for his trials and his blessings alike. In fact, to Paul they were the same thing!

"I thank my God every time I remember you," he wrote to the church members at Philippi" (Philippians 1:3).

"Ever since I heard about your faith in the Lord Jesus and your love for all the saints, I have not stopped giving thanks for you," he wrote to the Ephesians (1:15,16).

As we travel toward our life's dreams and aspirations, I believe our journey will be more satisfying—and enjoyable—if we remember to be thankful for the joys and opportunities that lie along the road. Being alert to those "side trips" can help us avoid the danger of focusing so narrowly on the goal that we fail to see God's blessings along the way, and fail to thank Him for them.

Cultivating a spirit of thankfulness has a twofold benefit: it helps us learn humility and fosters a sense of joy. Each experience, each relationship, each day that we are alive brings us opportunities to experience God in new ways. Even the difficult periods and the trying ordeals in our lives are opportunities to learn. We have countless unexpected chances to come to a deeper trust in God, to learn more about what we can be through Him and about what He would ultimately have us do with our lives.

One of the areas of my life in which I most fervently hope to be successful by God's standards is in rearing my son. Recently I was blessed with a small milestone on that journey.

Matthew (age 12) was studying for a science test. He was reviewing for me the material regarding cells as the basic unit of the human body. "Cells combine to make tissues, tissues combine to make organs, and organs combine to make systems," he recited.

"And where did the very first cell come from?" I asked him. I was anxious to see whether any of his teachers had been promoting a nonbiblical view of origins. But he had the right answer to my question.

"From God!" he said, looking at me with an *everybody*-knows-*that* expression.

At that moment I experienced a feeling of success. Somewhere, sometime during the past 12 years my son has come to understand that God is the Source and the Creator of all things. In that small accomplishment— that is, in creating an environment in which he could learn that basic principle—I have been successful. And I am very grateful for it.

When we remember to thank God for our blessings, our accomplishments, and even for the beginning of a new day, it helps us keep ourselves and our abilities in perspective. It gives us the chance to acknowledge again that all we are and have comes from God, lest we take ourselves too seriously or overrate our achievements.

At the same time, a spirit of thankfulness colors the way we look at the world; it enables us to view the glass as always being half full. We see the goodness of God, the evidence of His creative power, the loving-kindness with which He orders the universe. We see His hand in the sunset, in our child's "I love you," in a friend's encouraging word, in a job well done. We see life's promise, not its disappointments. We sense over and over again that He cares about us; then, secure in that assurance, we can ride out the day-to-day ups and downs with confidence—or at least with fortitude.

Even in our bleakest moments, when we see little for which to be grateful, we know that God is there. We can be thankful for His presence, thankful for the promise that He will sustain us when our human ability to endure runs out.

That knowledge alone gives us ample reason for gratitude.

SIGNPOST

For the LORD is good,
and his love endures forever;
his faithfulness continues
through all generations.

—Psalm 100:5

I Think I Can, I Think I Can...

Kathy's dream was to graduate from law school. She saw the needs of people who were intimidated by the legal system, who didn't have the education or the money to obtain legal services to protect their rights and their property. Someday, she hoped, she would work in a legal clinic, where she could help people in a concrete way. She freely admits to being an idealist who just wants to do her small part to bring more justice into the world.

For five years Kathy attended law school at night while working as a high school teacher during the day and (with her husband) caring for their two children.

"I don't think I can do this much longer," she would tell her husband, Jack, in her lowest moments of fatigue and discouragement. "It's just too much for one person. Teaching all day, grading papers, meeting with parents, and then going to classes after dinner, doing research in the library all weekend, staying up late every night—I just don't know if I can hang on. Maybe this isn't what God wants for me. Maybe it was a foolish idea."

Anyone who has ever had to work hard and long for something he or she wanted badly knows how Kathy felt. Sometimes, in the face of obstacles and limitations, the goal just seems impossible to reach. We feel our physical strength running out. Our mental and emotional energy seems sapped. We look around us at all the things we haven't gotten done—the house is a mess, our sister's birthday present is a month late being mailed, the Christmas cards are still unaddressed and it's March 12th—and we feel like failures. We feel inadequate to the task. Instead of feeling exhilarated by the challenge and inspired by the goal, we feel worn-out and discouraged.

That's where the biblical quality of perseverance comes in. The apostle Paul was an expert on this quality too. He not only demonstrated perseverance in his own life, but he constantly encouraged others to persevere in the face of opposition and despair. One of the most eloquently encouraging messages in all of Scripture occurs in his second letter to the Corinthian church. He wrote this about the ministry of the gospel:

"But we have this treasure in jars of clay to show that this all-surpassing power is from God and not from us. We are hard pressed on every side, but not crushed; perplexed, but not in despair; persecuted, but not abandoned; struck down, but not destroyed" (2 Corinthians 4:7-9).

We are the "jars of clay" containing God's treasure. It comes into the world only through us. If we give up, His work will not be done. If Kathy gave up, there would be one less person working to heal the effects of injustice in the world. If we decide that learning to understand and care about a co-worker instead of accepting a hostile truce is just too much effort, then we have made the world a less caring place. If we decide that resisting the sexual attraction of a male co-worker is just too hard, we'll fall easily into sin. If we decide that standing up for ethics and morality in the business world is too stressful, there will be one less voice crying out in the corporate wilderness.

"Let us not become weary in doing good," Paul wrote, "for at the proper time we will reap a harvest if we do not give up" (Galatians 6:9).

Remember when we talked about "doing enough," and the importance of making choices about where we will set the limits of our doing? In light of all that needs to be done for God's kingdom, I believe we face a daily challenge of sorting out the important from the trivial. We need to exercise judgment and discernment in deciding what is worth our time and energy and what isn't. We need to practice perseverance where it counts, and be willing to set limits elsewhere.

Perseverance doesn't mean being everything to everyone or doing everything that needs to be done. It means focusing on what is truly important and being willing to stay on course toward that important goal without being distracted by other things.

During some periods in our lives, like the five years Kathy spent in law school, we need to persevere to meet a concrete goal. We need to be willing to put off other goals and other needs in the interest of meeting that one goal. At other times in our lives, perseverance simply means not giving up on people or causes or efforts just because the going gets tough. Paul says we will reap a harvest if we do not give up. Surely we cannot succeed at anything if we aren't willing to practice perseverance.

The Hope of Glory

When I was in high school I attended a local Presbyterian church that had a Scottish minister—a burly, dark-haired man with piercing blue eyes who spoke with a thick Scottish accent. His sermons were those of a man on fire for the Lord. One of the most frequent phrases in his sermons and prayers was "in the hope of glory." Pronounced in his lilting accent and distinctive diction, the phrase sounded like "in the hope-eh of glaw-ry."

For me as a young person, there was magic in that phrase "the hope of glory." It was such a contrast with much that is around us—the humdrum, the routine, the plain, the tedious. Splendor is a such a rare thing.

God is glorious. He is magnificent, radiant, almighty, omniscient. Heaven, where we will be reunited with Him, will be glorious, too—splendid, beautiful beyond anything our minds can imagine. There we will be renewed, refreshed, and restored. The failures and tragedies of this life will be forgotten in the light of eternity. That's the hope of glory.

We need hope to succeed. We need the hope of glory, which gives us a heavenly perspective when earthly concerns seem unbearably complex. We need a simple, day-to-day kind of hope, too. Kathy hopes that her efforts to bring justice to others will make a difference. Cynthia hopes that with her nursing skills she'll be able to save a life or prevent a crippling injury. Cathy hopes that as a teacher she can be a positive influence in a child's life. Each of us hopes that we'll leave the world better than we found it, that we'll do something of value in our lives.

In working for a hospice, an organization that cares for terminally ill individuals and their families, I've had the opportunity to learn a great deal about hope. What hope does a dying person have when cure has been deemed impossible? The hope that tomorrow will be sunny. The hope that a grandchild will say his first word soon. The hope that a new medicine will relieve the pain more effectively. The hope that your husband or wife will find a deep reserve of courage to face the future without you. The hope that when death comes, you will greet it with a peaceful spirit, and that your loved ones will learn to live positively and optimistically without you. And, of course, the hope of a miracle by God's grace.

Hope is not a quality we pull out, like a formal gown or a sedate business suit, when the occasion calls for it. When we cultivate the quality of hope in our day-to-day lives, we live in expectation. We anticipate that God will work that day in our lives in a new way and that we will learn something precious and meaningful. We look ahead, not back. We face tomorrow with confidence that God has something important for us to do, and that in partnership with Him we will make it happen. Hope gives us the courage to pursue our goals and endure our setbacks and mistakes.

Paul calls hope "an anchor for the soul, firm and secure" (Hebrews 6:19). Hope anchors courage and feeds a willing heart; it fosters thankfulness and inspires perseverance. As Christians we can greet every day with hope, including the hope of satisfying and lasting success.

POINTS OF INTEREST

1. Do you need courage to face something specific in your life? What can you do to cultivate courage? Write a prayer below, asking God to help you learn courage to deal with the situation:

_____

_____

2. Can you have a willing heart in regard to serving God but not in regard to serving others, and vice versa? Can a person be a servant of God and of mankind without a willing heart? To what extent are you willing to use your talents and gifts from God to serve other people?

3. We all have so much for which to be thankful. Right now, list ten things in your life for which you are grateful, and thank God for them:

1. _____
2. _____
3. _____
4. _____
5. _____
6. _____
7. _____
8. _____
9. _____
10. _____

4. Think of a difficult situation facing you right now, and thank God for it. How does thanking God for it affect your feelings about the situation?

_____

_____

_____

5. How would you rate yourself on the "perseverance scale"? High? Low? If you are already a persevering person, why do you think that is the case? Are you more willing to persevere in some areas than others? If you are low on perseverance, what could you do to increase that quality in your life?

_____

_____

_____

6. What is your ultimate hope? Describe it below:

_____

_____

_____

_____

Now identify something you hope for today.

_____

_____

_____

What difference does hope make in your outlook?

_____

_____

SIGNPOST

*Restore to me the joy
of your salvation
and grant me a willing spirit,
to sustain me.*

—Psalm 51:12

*Hope does not disappoint us,
because God has poured out his love
into our hearts by the Holy Spirit,
whom he has given us.*

—Romans 5:5

PART FOUR

Are We There Yet?

CHAPTER 11

Setting a Personal Agenda

Whatever you can do,
or dream you can, begin it.
Boldness has genius, power,
and magic in it.

—Goethe

This is the hard part.

In the last ten chapters you've met a number of women like you, facing the same decisions, challenges, and dilemmas that you face; wanting the same things; as uncertain as you and I are about what success really means for a woman of God. You've read of their experiences, their work, their goals, their dreams. Now it's time to chart your own journey, to start discovering what that special brand of success which God has designed for *you* will look like.

The following pages constitute a book-within-a-book, a workbook designed to provide a personalized road map for your journey. May God bless you as you seek His will.

Charting a Course for Success

1. Right now, looking at my life as a whole, I would say I feel—
( ) Very successful
( ) Successful most of the time
( ) Fairly successful
( ) Successful only occasionally
( ) Not successful at all.

2. In specific areas of my life, I would rate my feeling of success as follows:

Job/Work
( ) Very successful
( ) Successful most of the time
( ) Fairly successful
( ) Successful only occasionally
( ) Not successful at all.

Home/Family
( ) Very successful
( ) Successful most of the time
( ) Fairly successful
( ) Successful only occasionally
( ) Not successful at all.

Non-Family Relationships
( ) Very successful
( ) Successful most of the time
( ) Fairly successful
( ) Successful only occasionally
( ) Not successful at all.

Spiritual Life/Relationship with God
( ) Very successful
( ) Successful most of the time
( ) Fairly successful
( ) Successful only occasionally
( ) Not successful at all.

Other (you select an area not mentioned above that's important to you)

_____

( ) Very successful
( ) Successful most of the time
( ) Fairly successful
( ) Successful only occasionally
( ) Not successful at all.

Are there still other areas of your life we haven't listed yet that you would like to include in this personal journey of success? If so, list them below and rate how successful you feel in them, using the same scale as in the previous questions.

Area   Rating

_____   _____

_____   _____

_____   _____

_____   _____

_____   _____

_____   _____

_____   _____

_____   _____

3. In the areas of your life in which you feel most successful, why do you think that is the case? Let's look at those areas.

For each area you rated as "very successful" or "successful most of the time," describe briefly what gives you that feeling of success. Think about factors such as feedback or approval from other people, internal satisfaction, personal accomplishment, and other factors that might contribute to your feeling of success in those areas.

Area   Reason for feeling of success

_____   _____

_____   _____

_____   _____

_____   _____

_____   _____

4. Now look at the remaining areas you rated as not giving you a very strong or frequent feeling of success. Try to identify what it is that makes you feel less successful in those areas.

Area   Reason for feeling unsuccessful

_____   _____

_____   _____

_____   _____

_____   _____

_____   _____

_____   _____

_____   _____

5. Do you think it is possible that one of the reasons you might feel unsuccessful in certain areas is that your definition of success isn't working? How do you define success for those areas? How are those definitions similar to or different from the way you define success in those areas where you feel more successful?

_____   _____
_____   _____
_____   _____

6. Refer to the definitions of success you wrote at the ends of Chapters 1, 7 and 8. Also reread the answer you wrote to question 7 at the end of Chapter 9. Now write a new definition that reflects what success means in your life (or copy a previous one that you feel is the best):

_____
_____
_____

7. List some areas of your life in which you would like to experience more success.

_____
_____
_____
_____
_____

Choose one of those areas you've listed above and complete the rest of these questions as they pertain to that one area. (You may want to repeat the process later for other areas, but it's less confusing for now to work with just one area.)

Identify your chosen area here:

_____

8. Based on your understanding of God's Word and on your experience of Him, what do you think He wants for you in this aspect of your life?

_____

_____

_____

9. Using the Work-Goals-Destination chart below, fill in the last column—the results you desire for that area of your life. Be sure to consider your answer to Questions 6 and 7 as you fill in the column. If it would be helpful, refer to the chart you completed at the end of Chapter 3, and also to the similar charts in Chapter 4.

Work (Route)	Goals (Milestones)	Destination (Desired results)

10. Which of the special gifts that God has given you do you think will help you the most in reaching the destination you've chosen?

_____

_____

_____

_____

11. As you think about your unique "package" of talents, abilities, skills, experiences, and knowledge, what are some special qualities or gifts in yourself that God can see but that those around you—or even you yourself—perhaps don't recognize? Is there some way you can cultivate and use those qualities more than you are presently doing? How do you think God wants you to use them?

Gift   Possible use

_____   _____

_____   _____

_____   _____

_____   _____

12. Now that you've filled in the destination on the chart and thought about your special gifts, choose some goals that, as you travel in partnership with God, will serve as milestones along the way. Choose a time frame for each goal. Add these to the chart.

13. As we discussed in Chapter 3, one of the dangers of becoming too focused on goals is losing sight of God's work in us along the way. What can you do to insure openness to God's presence and His leading as you progress on your journey? How can you keep the lines of communication with Him open? Describe here what you're going to do:

_____

_____

_____

_____

_____

_____

14. Now let's turn to the column labeled "Work" on the chart. The type of tasks you list here will depend on the life-area you chose as the topic of this exercise. List tasks related to your job outside the home if that's pertinent; you may also want to include other types of work: your home and family tasks, volunteer activities, tasks related to caring for friends or neighbors, etc. You decide what belongs in that space. Refer again to the completed

charts in the book if that's helpful. (If the life-area you identified in Question 7 as the topic for your Work-Goals-Destination chart is *not* related to your job outside the home, you may want to skip Question 14 for now and return to it later.)

15. Regardless of how you completed the "Work" column, let's reflect for a minute on your job situation.

Rate each of the items listed in the left-hand column on a 1-5 scale, with 5 being "This is almost always true of my job" and 1 being "This is almost never true of my job."

Almost never true				Almost always true
1	2	3	4	5

	True/Not True Rating
a. I feel successful in my work.	———
b. My job uses my talents and abilities.	———
c. I find the time I spend at work pleasant.	———
d. My work gives me opportunities for spiritual growth.	———
e. I am able to see my work as part of God's work in my life.	———
f. I am aware of God's presence when I'm at work.	———
g. I am proud to present my day's work to Him as an offering.	———
h. I have a sense that the work I do is important to the "big picture."	———

i. I learn from the people around me at work, even those with whom it's hard for me to get along. _____

j. I try to base my work-related decisions on God's standards rather than those of the workplace. _____

If you rated more than five of these areas "1" or "2," you might want to ask God to help you change either your work situation or the way you deal with it. We can't always change our situation in the way we'd like to, but we can always change our response to it, and God can always help us change both if we are willing to commit to partnership with Him. You might want to include in your chart a goal related to this kind of change, or you might want to complete another chart related specifically to seeking a greater sense of success in your work.

16. Now that you've completed the chart, let's go back to the goals you set. How will you know when you've met each goal—that is, when you have reached "enoughness" for that goal? Can it be measured in terms of—

- Having enough?
- Doing enough?
- Being enough?
- Knowing enough?

Looking at each of your goals, see which of the four "enoughness" categories they fall into. Then, for each goal, decide whether it can best be accomplished by—

a) Setting limits—for example, "To spend at least ten more minutes per day in the Scriptures" or "To stop taking work home more than one night a week."

b) Remaining "willingly dissatisfied"—that is, continually trying to improve (for example, in a certain skill or personal quality or relationship.)

Jot down an a) or a b) by each goal.

17. Remembering Christ's call to servanthood, now evaluate all three columns on the chart from that perspective. Do your tasks*, your goals, and your destination reflect a desire to serve God and others? Do you need to make revisions to the chart to reflect servanthood?

18. In Chapter 10 we talked about five qualities that the successful women and men of the Bible demonstrated: courage, a willing heart, thankfulness, perseverance, and hope. How is each of these related to the elements you've entered in your chart? Jot down some words or phrases in the table below to show how you can incorporate these qualities into your journey. The various qualities will probably be more closely related to certain elements of the chart than to others.

	How related to:		
Quality	Work	Goals	Destination
Courage			
A willing heart			
Thankfulness			
Perseverance			
Hope			

19. Review the "signpost" Bible verses at the end of each chapter. Select one or more that you feel best apply to the chart as you've completed it. Write that verse above the chart, and memorize it if you haven't already.

20. Stop now and offer a prayer to God regarding success in your life. Use your own words or, if you wish, the following prayer:

---

*In this case, consider not the tasks themselves but the way you approach them.

Dear God, I am excited about embarking on a journey toward greater success as a Christian woman. I know that I am successful in Your eyes simply because You love me, but I want to learn, grow, and mature in my walk with You. I believe You have called me to do great things for You, and I'm ready to respond to that call in a spirit of love and obedience. Be with me now, Lord, and in the days ahead as I explore Your glorious plan for me. Thank You for Your Son Jesus Christ, through whom You have made salvation possible. In His name, Amen.

Your destination is in view. Your milestones have been charted and your tasks laid out. May your journey be joyful and your discoveries exciting. You're off!

The harvest is plentiful but the workers are few. Ask the Lord of the harvest, therefore, to send out workers into his harvest field.
—Matthew 9:37,38

Other Good
Harvest House Reading

THE WORKING MOTHER'S GUIDE TO SANITY
by *Elsa Houtz*

Working mothers "have it all"—or do they? Written
from a down-to-earth, practical perspective, *The
Working Mother's Guide to Sanity* examines the most
fundamental concerns and problems working mothers
face.

Going beyond just identifying the problems, *The
Working Mother's Guide to Sanity* provides answers,
options, and solutions that work for the working
mother. Filled with heartwarming examples and
humorous anecdotes, Elsa Houtz shows the
sometimes-funny, sometimes-trying, and always-
challenging life of today's working mother.

IN GOD'S WORD
Devotional Studies to Enrich Your Life
with God's Truth
by *Nancie Carmichael*

Nancie Carmichael began her *personal* Bible study
years ago as a young pastor's wife. Today she is
the copublisher of *Virtue* magazine along with her
husband, Bill, and leads their over 130,000 subscribers
in a Bible study each month. *In God's Word* is the
compilation of the years of diligent effort and care
Nancie has brought to the Bible study column of
Virtue. Embark on a great *personal* adventure as you
get to know the Lord more intimately through daily
time in His Word.

SURVIVAL FOR BUSY WOMEN
Establishing Efficient Home Management
by *Emilie Barnes*

A hands-on manual for establishing a more efficient home-management program. Over 25 charts and forms can be personalized to help you organize your home.

WORKING AT HOME
by *Lindsey O'Connor*

What are mothers (or fathers) to do when they want to stay home with their children and yet need additional income to make ends meet? Home businesses are sprouting up all over the country as more and more people are finding a way to combine parenting and working without having to give up traditional family roles.

In *Working at Home*, Lindsey O'Connor helps you determine whether a home business is for you and how you can get one off the ground.

WHERE WILL I FIND THE TIME?
Making Time Work For You
by *Sally McClung*

For most of us, the busier our lives become the less fulfilled we seem to be. *Where Will I find the Time?* offers realistic advice to everyone who wants to learn to use time more effectively.

Sally McClung shares her biblically-based insights for successfully prioritizing the demands of marriage, family, and work while still leaving opportunities for recreation and renewal. McClung provides encouragement to those who struggle with life management and personal organization skills and gives practical information that can increase your effectiveness.

Dear Reader:

We would appreciate hearing from you regarding this Harvest House nonfiction book. It will enable us to continue to give you the best in Christian publishing.

1. What most influenced you to purchase *The Working Woman's Guide to Real Success*?
   - ☐ Author
   - ☐ Subject matter
   - ☐ Backcover copy
   - ☐ Recommendations
   - ☐ Cover/Title
   - ☐ _____

2. Where did you purchase this book?
   - ☐ Christian bookstore
   - ☐ General bookstore
   - ☐ Department store
   - ☐ Grocery store
   - ☐ Other

3. Your overall rating of this book:
   ☐ Excellent ☐ Very good ☐ Good ☐ Fair ☐ Poor

4. How likely would you be to purchase other books by this author?
   - ☐ Very likely
   - ☐ Somewhat likely
   - ☐ Not very likely
   - ☐ Not at all

5. What types of books most interest you?
   (check all that apply)
   - ☐ Women's Books
   - ☐ Marriage Books
   - ☐ Current Issues
   - ☐ Self Help/Psychology
   - ☐ Bible Studies
   - ☐ Fiction
   - ☐ Biographies
   - ☐ Children's Books
   - ☐ Youth Books
   - ☐ Other _____

6. Please check the box next to your age group.
   - ☐ Under 18
   - ☐ 18-24
   - ☐ 25-34
   - ☐ 35-44
   - ☐ 45-54
   - ☐ 55 and over

Mail to: Editorial Director
Harvest House Publishers
1075 Arrowsmith
Eugene, OR 97402

Name _____

Address _____

City _____ State _____ Zip _____

Thank you for helping us to help you in future publications!